Praise for

WHEN I CONSIDER YOUR HEAVENS

Drawing on contemporary philosophy and science, Dr. Latham has written an accessible and lively introduction to a wide range of reasons for diagnosing the Universe as God's creation.

—**Peter S. Williams**, author of *A Universe from Someone: Essays on Natural Theology (Wipf and Stock, 2022)*

***

In succinct prose, Dr. Antony Latham summarizes the compelling reasons given by science and philosophy for the existence of God. I heartily recommend it to anyone who is wondering about this most important question of our lives.

—**Michael J. Behe**, author of *Darwin's Black Box*

***

An excellent primer on the many reasons why advances in science and our human experience of moral feelings and beauty point us to the existence of God.

—**Dr Trevor Stammers**, author of *The Ethics of Global Organ Acquisition: Moral Arguments about Transplantation* and co-editor of *The Ethics of Generating Post-humans*, *Bloomsbury*

WHEN I CONSIDER
YOUR HEAVENS

How Science and Philosophy

Lead Us to God

Antony Latham

Published by KHARIS PUBLISHING, imprint of
KHARIS MEDIA LLC.

Copyright © 2025 Antony Latham

ISBN-13: 978-1-63746-370-3

ISBN-10: 1-63746-370-7

Library of Congress Control Number: 2025945754

All KHARIS PUBLISHING products are available at
special quantity discounts for bulk purchases for sales
promotions, premiums, fund-raising, and educational
needs. For details, contact:

Kharis Media LLC
Tel: 1-630-909-3405
support@kharispublishing.com
www.kharispublishing.com

*When I consider your heavens, the work of your fingers,
the moon and the stars, which you have set in place,
what is man that you are mindful of him, and the son
of man that you care for him?*

Psalm 8:3-4

TABLE OF CONTENTS

INTRODUCTION

It was not long ago that the vast majority of people in the Western world took it for granted that some form of God existed[1]. It seemed perfectly rational for intelligent people to assume there must be a Creator. How else could one explain the existence of everything?

The Scientific Revolution took place in this environment. It was belief in a Creator that gave rise to the quest to understand nature. Indeed, this thirst for knowledge was considered part of worship. There was a sense that God was pleased when we worked to understand the laws of nature and the cosmos. The greatest scientists of this era of discovery were people of devout faith. They included Kepler, Copernicus, Galileo, Newton, Leibniz, and later, Faraday, Cuvier, Herschel, Agassiz, Mendel, and Clerk Maxwell, to name but a few.

Yet, something extraordinary happened. A strain of the Enlightenment philosophy emerged in the 17th and 18th centuries, which gradually led to an undermining of

---

[1] As described in Taylor, Charles (2018). A Secular Age. Belknap Press.

faith in God. The very knowledge of the world that had been painstakingly and brilliantly explored by believers was given as a reason to doubt. Only human reason and empirical knowledge were valid paths to truth. As we came to understand more and more, we became proud of our knowledge. We worked out how the planets moved, and how the sun shone. We understood chemistry and the behaviour of molecules. We harnessed electricity and built amazing machines. It seemed that, by understanding so much, we no longer needed anything supernatural to explain it all. We effectively short-circuited God, removing him from our worldview.

Then came Darwin, the reluctant and anxious agnostic, who seemed to pull the rug from under our assumptions about life. A spirit of disbelief grew, and his acolytes continue, even now, to blow cold on our efforts to bring God back in.

Of course, there is the possibility that the doubters are right. Perhaps there is now no evidence of God. We have not found him in the galaxies or the particle accelerators. Where is His signature? Everything is physical and only the material exists, say the New Atheists. My aim in this book is to expose this view as patently false.

It is not my job to explain exactly why this atmosphere of doubt pervades the western mind. It is partly hubris—we know so much now, don't we? It is partly our increased wealth—we are comfortable, and life is no longer short and brutish; so, we don't need God anymore.

It is also a particularly "left-brained" view of things. As so ably described by Iain McGilchrist[2], we have abandoned the part of us that sees the whole picture and the truth behind the details. Instead, we try so hard to analyse and focus on the wood that we don't even recognise that there are such things as trees.

It is also, as I will try to explain later, the firm but unfounded belief that the universe is causally closed—that nothing non-physical from outside can have effect. This pervasive faithlessness is not based on reason, and exposing this is the purpose of this book.

I will argue that it is also a form of intellectual laziness. In the study of cosmology, philosophy, consciousness, biology, morality, beauty and the phenomenon of free-will, we are compelled to come to a conclusion that the grand narrative of materialism has failed. It is the great myth of our time- the wool pulled over our eyes.

The stakes are high. If there is no Creator then there is no ultimate meaning. We are mere accidental and ultimately purposeless products of a blind universe.

Stay with me and see how fundamentally wrong this is. Far from being a hindrance to faith, science and philosophy lead us to a very reasoned belief.

I trust that, by examining the evidence, readers will not simply conclude that a Creator exists, but also recognise that God's character shines through the facts.

---

[2] McGilchrist, Iain (2023). The Matter with Things: Our Brains, Our Delusions, and the Unmaking of the World. Perspectiva.

The goodness and beauty that we aspire to, and often find, are part of God's very nature.

In showing the evidence of God's existence, I do not imply that we can only come to faith through such evidence. On the contrary, I believe that faith in God is a *Properly Basic Belief*[3] that all of us have naturally. May the evidence I put forward lead us back to this.

I hope the readers will enjoy this book in its entirety. However, individual chapters can also be read independently for those seeking an overview of a particular area.

---

[3] As described by Alvin Plantinga in: Plantinga, A. (2000) Warranted Christian Belief. Oxford University Press

CHAPTER 1

COSMOLOGICAL REASONS TO BELIEVE IN GOD

Astrophysics has expanded our understanding of the universe in ways that leave us quite stunned. We live in a cosmos far more immense and interesting than we could have ever imagined. It is also extraordinarily beautiful, as the photos from the Hubble telescope vividly show. Where is God in this? A person with a materialist mind-set might argue that our increased knowledge pushes God into the background—after all, we have plumbed the depths of space and found no trace of Him. Or have we?

There was a beginning

Many readers, even as children, have at times wondered why anything exists at all. Why is there something rather than nothing? This is a not a trivial question, and I hope to explore where it leads.

The very first words of the bible state:

"In the beginning God created the heavens and the earth."[4]

One of the keys to understanding creation is to examine this beginning. The question is: Was there an *actual* beginning of the universe? If there was a definite beginning (as the Bible tells us) then we are obliged to ask how it occurred. Several facts show that there *was* indeed a beginning. Moreover, we will see that the universe came from nothing physical—no material 'stuff' set it in motion. What can we conclude? There must be a non-physical cause. Let us examine the evidence.

The expansion of the universe

In 1927, Georges Lemaître, a Belgian catholic priest and a brilliant mathematician, discovered that the universe is expanding. Using Einstein's equations of relativity,

---

[4] Genesis 1:1

Lemaître showed that the universe must be growing in size. Until then, most scientists, including Einstein, believed that the universe was static. As a result, the findings of Lemaître were initially doubted and rejected. Einstein himself rejected the idea at first, but later acknowledged that Lemaître was correct and endorsed his conclusions.

Incidentally, Lemaître never felt that discoveries in cosmology conflicted with his belief in God as Creator.

In 1929, astronomer Edwin Hubble confirmed this expansion through observation, using the Mount Wilson observatory telescope, the best at the time. Hubble found that light from distant galaxies is 'redshifted,' indicating that they are moving away from us.

To explain redshift, it is helpful to think of our experience of the change of pitch in sound when a car comes towards us and then recedes. We all know that as it recedes, the pitch lowers. This happens because the sound waves reaching our ears are elongated because they come from a receding source. Similarly, if a light source is moving away from us, the light wavelengths are perceived to be longer. Longer wavelengths move the light towards the red end of the spectrum. Hubble observed that the light from almost all galaxies beyond our own is redshifted, indicating that they are receding in all directions. He also noted that the farther away the galaxies are, the faster they are receding.

One possible way to visualise this phenomenon is to think of a cake baked with raisins scattered throughout it. As the cake expands, the raisins on the outside (representing galaxies) move away from the centre faster than those in the middle.

You may wonder how astronomers were able to determine the distance to galaxies, so far away. There is a type of star, known as a Cepheid variable, which periodically changes its brightness. It is possible to work out the distance to a Cepheid variable star by observing the pattern of its brightness variations and the actual amount of light we receive from it. A remarkable but less well-known scientist, Henrietta Swan Leavitt, used a telescope in 1908 to observe thousands of these variable stars to demonstrate the accuracy of this method for measuring cosmic distance. Leavitt, a devout Christian, was nominated for a Nobel Prize in 1925, but sadly, she died before the award. This was the first reliable way to determine the distance to galaxies.

Because the universe is expanding, Lemaître and others realised that there must have been an initial, extremely dense and hot state when this expansion began. To many scientists, this seemed uncomfortably similar to an act of creation, which conflicted with their naturalistic philosophy. They somewhat derogatorily called it the "Big Bang" – a name that stuck. Thus, the expansion of the universe is one reason we believe there was a beginning - the Big Bang.

Entropy leads us to assume a beginning

Entropy is a scientific term for randomness or disorder in any system and is the basis for the second law of thermodynamics. In a closed system, entropy *always* increases over time. Another definition is that entropy describes the degradation of the matter and energy in the universe to an ultimate state of inert uniformity. For example, heat from a cup of coffee dissipates into the surrounding air, leaving the coffee at the same uniform temperature as the surroundings.

Entropy is like a clock; it is time-dependent and increases with time. The universe currently has a particular overall entropy, which increases every second. From this, we can infer that there was a time when entropy was at its minimum at the beginning. The second law of thermodynamics implies an actual beginning when the universe's entropy was near zero, at a minimum.

The Big Bang, often mentioned casually, should leave us in awe. Cosmologists say that in the earliest stages of the Big Bang, the entire universe, all the matter and energy that we have today, was compressed into a volume smaller than an atom. The temperature just seconds after the Big Bang event happened is estimated at 10^{32} degrees Celsius (that is 10 followed by 32 zeros).

Cosmic background radiation

In 1948, cosmologists Alpher and Herman theorised that the Big Bang should have left behind a detectable afterglow or radiation. It was a rather fortunate pair of scientists called Penzias and Wilson who first detected this in 1964.[5]

They were doing something else entirely, building a detector of radio waves for satellite communication and they noticed a constant interference. After carefully reducing every possible cause of this, there continued to be a background "noise" of microwave radiation from all directions. Remarkably, the strength of this radiation matched the predictions made for the Big Bang. Penzias and Wilson received a Nobel Prize for this discovery.

Those old enough to remember analogue TV sets may recall the annoying 'white noise' often experienced. About 1% of this was caused by the cosmic background radiation. It is quite amazing to realise that, billions of years later, we are still surrounded by the radiation emitted from that unimaginably powerful event.

This discovery of cosmic background radiation strongly supports the Big Bang theory and a literal beginning of the universe.

---

[5] Lemos, P. and Shah, S. (2024). The Cosmic Microwave Background and H0. In Di Valentino, E. and Brout, D. (Eds). The Hubble Constant Tension. Springer

The impossibility of an infinite age to the universe

There are sound mathematical reasons why the universe cannot be infinitely old and must have had a beginning.

Great thinkers over the ages have argued for what Aristotle called a 'Prime Mover' to account for the creation of the universe[6].

The Islamic scholar Al-Ghazali stated:

"Every being which begins has a cause for its beginning; now the world is a being which begins; therefore, it possesses a cause for its beginning."[7]

Thomas Aquinas identified this cause as God in his great 13th century work, *Summa Theologica*.[8]

More recently, philosopher William Lane Craig has argued persuasively for God being the First Cause of all that exists.[9] One of the chief reasons for holding to this view is that there is no such thing as an actual infinite series of things.

---

[6] Aristotle (1941). "Physics." In The Basic Works of Aristotle (Different font), edited by Richard McKeon. New York: Random House Reprint ed., Modern Library, 2001.

[7] Al-Ghazali (1962). Kitab al lqtisad. Ankara: University of Ankara Press. pp. 15–16.

[8] Aquinas, Thomas. Summa Theologica: Treatise on the Creation. Great books of the Western World edition. pp. 238

[9] https://www.reasonablefaith.org/writings/popular-writings/existence-nature-of-god/the-kalam-cosmological-argument

The celebrated mathematician David Hilbert asserted: *"The infinite is nowhere to be found in reality...the role that remains for the infinite is solely that of an idea".*[10]

There are two types of infinity: potential infinity and actual infinity. Potential infinity is used in many mathematical equations, while actual infinity involves real things. This is so important because some people propose an infinitely old universe (or even a series of universes). Atheists often make this argument to reject the notion of a creative beginning. But is an eternal universe that stretches back infinitely in time truly possible? This is where the knowledge of infinity becomes useful.

Imagine trying to add grains of sand to a heap. Perhaps you continue to do this until the heap is bigger than the known universe. No matter how long you do this, there would still be a finite number of grains in the heap. With each addition, the number increases by one. There could never be an infinite number of grains of sand. It is the same if you begin counting from one and continue indefinitely; you will never actually reach infinity.

Therefore, infinity cannot be achieved by successive addition of anything. Likewise, successive additions of moments in time or physical causes can never amount to an infinite time or number of causes. Time is considered to be a fourth dimension and part of the physical 'stuff' of our cosmos, just like those grains of

---

[10] Hilbert, David. (1924). He made this statement in a lecture.

sand, an infinite length of time cannot exist in our universe.

Another way to understand this is to consider whether it is possible to traverse infinity. Imagine yourself in a very fast rocket travelling at the speed of light and aimed at a star that is an infinite distance away. Would you ever reach it? The answer is no. This is because no matter how fast you go or the number of years you go, you would always be an infinite distance away from such an imaginary star.

Or think of a well that is infinitely deep with a ladder going all the way down. If you were to imagine starting to climb out of the well from an infinite distance down, you would never reach the top.

Similarly, if there was an actual infinite past, it would be impossible to reach the present from such a 'time'. Yet, we are certainly here in the present, which means time does not stretch back infinitely. Therefore, there must have been a beginning.

Everything that is physical must, therefore, have a beginning. This includes any possible series of universes, an idea some people hold. After all, a series of universes or Big Bangs still amounts to successive causal events. As we have seen, it is impossible to have an infinite series of anything, including such causal events.

We can thus confidently say that the universe had an actual beginning.

The principle of sufficient reason

As we have already hinted, perhaps the greatest philosophical question ever is: Why is there something rather than nothing? We live in a universe, but why does it exist at all? Could there not simply be nothing, no things or time or space? But there is something.

Does everything exist as a brute fact, with no reason apart from itself? This is the predominant atheist position. Many atheists resist the idea that there is a cause of everything that is not itself physical. In other words, they reject any notion of a non-physical cause of the universe.

Yet, common sense tells us that any physical thing, or collection of such things, needs an explanation. That explanation cannot be itself.

Gottfried Leibniz (1646-1716), whom Bertrand Russell called "one of the greatest intellects of all time",[11] wrote about 'the principle of sufficient reason'. In one of his writings, he considered an object such as a book and wrote:

What is true of these books is also true of the different states of the world (his word for universe) for the state which follows is, in a sense, copied from a previous state, though in accordance with certain laws of change. And so, however far we go back into previous states, we will never find in those states a complete

---

[11] Russell, Bertrand (1946). History of Western Philosophy. Edition (1961). Routledge, pp. 563

explanation for why, indeed, there is any world at all, and why it is the way it is.[12]

Leibniz concluded that there must be an explanation for the universe, and that this explanation lies outside the universe itself. This explanation does not require any further justification for the existence of God, who is a necessary being.

I have never encountered any philosopher who has successfully refuted Leibniz on this issue. Of course, there have been various objections to this and we will look at some of these now.

Objections

1. While it is true that everything that exists within the universe needs an explanation, the universe is an exception.

It is not clear why the universe should be an exception to this rule. In fact, the objection is based on a worldview, that only physical things and causes exist, rather than any sound reasoning.

2. How could God exist without an explanation? Who created God?

Richard Dawkins, in his book *The God Delusion* strongly present this objection, along with many other atheists.[13]

---

[12] See at: https://plato.stanford.edu/entries/sufficient-reason/
[13] Dawkins, R. (2006). The God Delusion. Bantam Press.

Firstly, God is not subject to the laws of the universe because He is not part of the universe. As the Bible explains, God is spirit, not physical. Of course, we maintain that He added a human nature to His divine nature in the physical form of God the Son, Jesus, but God Himself is not part of the physical universe. Therefore, He is exempt from the rules of physical cause and effect.

Secondly, we know that time itself is part of the physical universe, but God exists outside of time. There is no 'before' God; He is eternal. While we may not fully understand this, it makes perfect sense. We are reminded of the verse from the second letter of Peter:[14]

With the Lord one day is as a thousand years, and a thousand years as a day.

Thirdly, as we have already seen, there is no such thing as an infinite series of causes. This means there had to be an *uncaused cause* of everything.

Thus, science and philosophy confirm what the verse in Genesis states; there was indeed a beginning. We can also confirm through simple logic that the cause of that beginning must be non-physical (not part of the universe) and uncaused: God.

Creation from nothing?

The verse in Genesis requires us to say that the universe was created from nothing. This is because if there were

---

[14] 2 Peter 2:8

already some existing physical "stuff" from which God created everything, it would not be a true beginning. It would simply be a *rearrangement* of what was already there.

It has long been a central tenet of Judaeo-Christian theology that the universe was created from nothing, a doctrine known as *creatio ex nihilo*. What does science tell us about this?

Remarkably, most cosmologists agree that the universe came into existence from nothing. This is not because they all believe in God, but rather because of their cosmological conclusions and analyses of the Big Bang point to this origin.

Of course, this poses a challenge for atheists: how could everything come from nothing without invoking the supernatural? This is where the discussion by twists and turns gets interesting as we read the conclusions of well-known atheist cosmologists. Such scientists try to smuggle in something physical which already exists.

A great example is the late Stephen Hawking, probably the most celebrated scientist of his generation. He agreed that the universe came from nothing but consider what he says about it in his book *The Grand Design*:

> *Because there is a law such as gravity, the universe can and will create itself from nothing…spontaneous creation is the reason why there is something rather than nothing, why the universe*

exists, why we exist. It is not necessary to invoke God to light the blue touch paper and set the universe going.[15]

Hawking was an extraordinary scientist, but here his reasoning falls short. He claims the universe came from nothing, yet in the same sentence acknowledges the existence of laws such as gravity. He makes no attempt to explain why the law of gravity or other physical laws were already in place. Such laws are not nothing. In fact, this represents a significant lapse in judgement from a great mind. It does make one wonder how far the atheist will go to avoid the inevitable conclusion.

Hawking is not alone in this. A typical example is physicist Laurence Krauss, who wrote a book titled *A Universe from Nothing*[16]. His explanation for how about the universe arose from nothing is that a quantum field fluctuation set it all in motion. A quantum field fluctuation is indeed a real thing in quantum physics. Within quantum fields, particles can appear seemingly out of nowhere into existence. So why does this not support the atheist position?

A particle (or a universe) coming into existence within a quantum field is not doing so from nothing because it requires energy. Mass and energy in the universe are inextricably linked, as Einstein showed in the famous equation $E=MC^2$. There is no such thing as a free lunch, nor a free particle without some energy.

---

[15] Hawking, S. (2010). The Grand Design Bantam Press. Pp. 180
[16] Krauss, L. (2012). A Universe from Nothing: why there is something rather than nothing. Simon & Schuster, UK

Therefore, Krauss is completely wrong in asserting that a quantum fluctuation could create the universe without enormous amounts of pre-existing energy. You cannot have it both ways: claiming the universe came from nothing while simultaneously relying on something.

I once debated an atheist astronomer at a university meeting. He agreed that all the evidence points to the universe coming from nothing. When I asked how this could be without God, he argued that the quantum field contained both negative and positive energy, which, if they cancel each other out, would amount to nothing. I challenged him to explain why positive or a negative energy should be considered 'nothing'. He was unable to provide an answer.

That first verse in Genesis is worth repeating:

In the beginning, God created the heavens and the earth

Science and philosophy faithfully back up the truth of these few words.

CHAPTER 2

A FINE-TUNED UNIVERSE

We now understand a great deal about the conditions of the universe just after the Big Bang. For a universe capable of supporting life, those conditions had to be exquisitely precise. In this chapter, I will show some of the ways the forces and physical laws at that primordial time must have been designed to be that way. Stay with me as I explain some of these conditions.

Is it all accidental, as the atheists insist, or is there a strong case for a Creator behind these conditions? Richard Dawkins said in a 2022 Premier Radio interview regarding this: *"If someone was going to convince me of the need for a God, it would be there."* [17]

As I discuss the initial state of the universe, I will use a fair number of scientific terms. If you are not a scientist, please scan the points- you will still understand the overall argument.

Unevenness of the expanding energy

At the very beginning, just microseconds after the Big Bang, there was a slight unevenness in the expanding energy. If it had been totally uniform, there would have been no coalescence into galaxies. Instead, the universe would have been homogenous and featureless.

Because of this slight irregularity, matter was able to clump together into structures such as stars. The amplitude of these irregularities has been calculated and is referred to as Q. Q had to be close to 0.0001. If it had been increased minutely, the universe would have collapsed in a big 'crunch'. If it had been decreased slightly, the universe would have contained no structures, no galaxies, no stars, and no life. [18]

---

[17] https://www.premierunbelievable.com/unbelievable/did-we-hear-richard-dawkins-swansong-to-new-atheism/13205.article
[18] Rees, Sir Martin (2003). Our Cosmic Habitat W & N.

Matter vs Antimatter

It is believed that matter and antimatter were originally present in exactly the same quantities and therefore should have annihilated each other, leaving just energy behind.

However, Andrei Sakharov, the Russian physicist, showed that there is a very slight asymmetry between the two, favouring matter over antimatter. This difference is just one part in a billion. Sir Martin Rees, the Astronomer Royal, wrote: "*We owe our existence to a difference in the ninth decimal place.*"[19]

Gravitational constant

If the value of the gravitational constant differed by even the slightest amount- more than 1 in 10^{60} (1 followed by 60 zeros), in either direction- the universe would either have expanded too rapidly to form stars or would have collapsed in on itself.

Expansion rate of the universe

The expansion rate of the universe depends on what is known as the *cosmological constant*. This constant represents the balance between the attractive force of gravity and the repulsive force of the Big Bang. The cosmological constant must be extremely close to zero. Steven Weinberg, Nobel laureate in physicist, stated at

---

[19] Rees, Sir Martin (2003). Our Cosmic Habitat W & N.

a university conference in 2000 that if this constant differed by more than 1 in 10^{120}, the universe would either expand too rapidly or too slowly. In either case, there would be no stars and no life.[20] This remarkable fact is widely accepted by the majority of physicists.

Ratio of strong nuclear force to electromagnetic force

If the ratio of the nuclear strong force to the electromagnetic force differed by more than 1 part in 10^{16}, there would be no stars producing the elements necessary for life.[21]

Ratio of the electromagnetic constant to the gravitational force constant

These constants must be precisely balanced. If the ratio increased by one part in 10^{40}, only small stars would form. If it decreased by one part in 10^{40}, only large stars would form.

We need both large and small stars to make life possible. Small stars burn long enough to support planets where life can develop, while large stars are necessary to produce the elements essential for life.

.

[20] Weinberg, Steven. See his article on this in Skeptical Inquirer Sept./Oct. 2001, p.67.
[21] https://explainingscience.org/2022/06/14/our-finely-tuned-universe-part-ii-examples-of-fine-tuning/

Paul Davies writes that this precision is like a *"marksman hitting a coin at the far side of the universe."*[22]

Resonance energy of carbon

Carbon, which is essential for life, is created in stars. It is fair to say we are made of stardust.

Astrophysicists Fred Hoyle and Edwin Salpeter discovered that the formation of carbon in stars depends on a particular feature – a mode of vibration, or resonance, of the carbon atom with a specific energy level. If this energy were to change by more than 1% in either direction, no carbon could form.

Hoyle wrote:

A common sense interpretation of the facts suggests that a super intellect has monkeyed with physics as well as with chemistry and biology, and that there are no blind forces worth speaking about in nature.[23]

Odds of getting a low entropy start

This fine-tuning surpasses all others in its precision. A low-entropy beginning of the universe (see the discussion on entropy in the last chapter) is essential for the second law of thermodynamics. Roger Penrose has shown that for this to occur there had to be a specific

---

[22] Davies, P. (1983). God and the New Physics. Weidenfeld & Nicolson.

[23] Hoyle, F. (1982). The Universe – Past and Present Reflections. Annual Review of Astronomy and Astrophysics. Vol 20, p.16

volume of what is called 'phase space'. This had to be accurate to one part in 10^{10} to the power 123. This number is so large that it far exceeds the number of particles in the universe.

In his book *The Emperor's New Mind*, Penrose writes: "This tells us how precisely the Creator's aim must have been, namely to an accuracy of one part power 10^{10} to the power 123."[24]

Regarding all these fine-tuning facts—and this is just a sample—Stephen Hawking wrote: "*The remarkable fact is that the value of these numbers seems to have been very finely adjusted to make possible the development of life.*"[25]

Freeman Dyson, the legendary physicist, said: "*I do not feel like an alien in this universe. The more I examine the universe and study the details of its architecture, the more evidence I find that the universe in some sense knew we were coming.*"[26]

Objections

Some object by arguing that any complex system or large collection of objects naturally involves highly unlikely complexity. According to this view, we should expect extremely improbable conditions at the start of any universe. In other words, theists like me are merely creating a false impression of design. All systems are

---

[24] Penrose, R. (1989). The Emperor's New Mind. Oxford University Press, p. 344

[25] Hawking, S. (1988). A Brief History of Time. Bantam

[26] Freeman Dyson (1979). Disturbing the Universe. New York: Harper and Row.

complex, and no assemblage of matter and energy is exactly the same as any other. Therefore, the appearance of fine-tuning could simply be due to chance.

This view, held by some very intelligent people, fails to distinguish between *normal complexity* and *specified complexity*. Let me explain with an analogy.

Imagine a pile of Scrabble tiles. If I throw them on the floor, they form a particular arrangement. That exact pattern is astronomically unlikely to repeat- I could throw them a billion times and never recreate that pattern. This represents the atheist's perspective: any universe arrangement is inherently improbable, so why invoke design?

Now consider this: I throw the tiles again, creating another random pattern. I leave for coffee and return ten minutes later to find a new arrangement spelling out: "Dad is very messy and should not throw Scrabble on the floor."

This is *specified complexity*. I immediately know one of my children arranged the tiles. Why? The pattern isn't just statistically improbable-it's functionally specified. It conveys a meaningful message.

We apply this same logic in other disciplines. When an archaeologist unearths a stone with markings, they determine whether these are random natural patterns or evidence of design. If the markings form recognisable symbols or patterns, we conclude that they are deliberately designed-not random arrangements.

There is a long-standing programme to look for evidence of alien life, SETI – the Search for Extraterrestrial Intelligence. By examining radio emissions from distant stars, the scientists are looking for evidence of design. So far, the only radio emissions are obviously from known physical objects and have no evidence of design; complex but not specified for intelligence. Now imagine receiving a series of radio signals that transmit the first 100 prime numbers in perfect sequence. We would immediately recognise this as the work of an intelligence. That is an example of specified complexity.

We know that the only possible conditions which could lead to life on earth were present at the Big Bang. Out of trillions upon trillions upon trillions of possibilities, only those exact conditions would do. It is not simply complex but is precisely *specified* for life. This is why we conclude that it can only be the result of intelligence.

Multiple Universes?

Most cosmologists agree that there is something amazing about this tuning and it cannot be dismissed.

One way to avoid concluding that there is a Creator is to propose the idea of multiple universes. Perhaps our universe is just one among countless universes. This would mean that, given enough universes, the right conditions could occur in at least one of them, and we are simply fortunate to be in that particular universe. You can see the reasoning here: no need for design, just chance.

However, firstly, there is no physical evidence for the existence of other universes. Secondly, this idea is principally ideological rather than scientific. In other words, it is proposed mainly to counter belief in a creator. This is a philosophical and religious position, not one grounded in science. It is a 'world view', not a scientific theory.

Though illustrations are always imperfect, this idea is similar to throwing millions of pieces of Scrabble which I throw trillions of times, hoping to randomly produce the complete works of Shakespeare perfectly arranged on the floor, with every dot and comma in place.

Yet, there is zero evidence for such a scenario, and it is based on an *a priori* assumption that there is no creator.

As the philosopher William of Ockham showed, the best explanation is usually the simplest one, requiring the least alteration of known facts.

By the way, as discussed in the previous chapter, even if multiple universes existed, that collection would still constitute a single overall physical entity. This entity must have had a beginning and a cause for that beginning-something beyond the multiple universes themselves.

Man's arrogance?

Some might argue that the claim we are somehow special and that the universe was fine-tuned is mere arrogance. In other words, that we are boasting about how important humans are.

Firstly, the fine-tuning is not just for humanity; it applies to the possibility of any life at all.

Secondly, we are simply examining the facts and evidence. We are not exaggerating this evidence to make ourselves seem more important.

God of the gaps?

Some argue that we are simply inserting God into the gaps in our current knowledge, and that this reflects ignorance. They claim that once we know more, the idea of God will be eliminated. This argument is somewhat derogatorily known as "God of the gaps".

However, it is the *increase* in knowledge about the universe that leads us to belief in design and a Creator, not ignorance. This is quite the opposite of the "God of the gaps" argument.

John Lennox, Professor of Mathematics at the University of Oxford, writes: *"We should note that the preceding arguments are not 'God of the gaps' arguments; it is advances in science, not ignorance of science, that have revealed this fine tuning to us. In that sense, there is no 'gap' in the science. The question is rather: how should we interpret the science? In what direction is it pointing?"*[27] His conclusion is that science overwhelmingly provides evidence for a designer of the universe.

---

[27] Lennox, J. (2009). God's undertaker: has science buried God? Lion Hudson.

The universe is remarkably and finely tuned to allow for life on our planet. This is no accident; it is specifically designed. All the evidence points in this direction, and we can conclude that only an extraordinary mind could have achieved this. This mind must be beyond our comprehension of immense ability, power, artistry, and purpose.

Not only this, such a Creator perfectly aligns with biblical theism: a God who can intimately interact with and be involved in every aspect of creation.

CHAPTER 3

THE BEGINNING OF LIFE

In 2005, I wrote a book presenting the scientific evidence for the design in biology[28]. It includes a chapter about the first life on earth. I can safely say that since then, almost 20 years ago, there has been no significant advancement in explaining the origin of life. In fact, as we know more about the complexity of the simplest cell, the goalposts have moved even further away.

---

[28] Latham, Antony. (2005). The Naked Emperor: Darwinism Exposed. Janus

Earth is at least 4.8 billion years old. At that time, our planet was a hot and hostile place. There was no solid crust, and it was continuously bombarded by stray 'bits' of material circling the sun. It is thought by many that our moon was formed from a large chunk of earth, propelled into space by a collision from a Mars-sized object.

The earliest evidence of life comes from ancient rocks found in Greenland, which shows a smoking-gun signature of what is likely to have been life. These rocks are 3.8 billion years old and contain a slight excess of carbon 12 relative to carbon 13 - a characteristic of photosynthetic carbon fixation.

There is also evidence of fossil bacteria in rock formations in Australia known as the Apex Chert. These microscopic fossils have been dated to approximately 3.46 billion years old. The dating is based on the known decay rate of Uranium-238 into Lead-206 within these rocks.

Very soon, therefore, after earth formed, geologically speaking, there is strong evidence that bacteria were already present. This time frame should give us pause for thought. Bacteria are incredibly complex organisms, and those found in what is now Australia used photosynthesis, a highly sophisticated method of converting sunlight energy.

The humble bacterium is far more complex than any conceivable man-made object. I like the description by Paul Davies[29]:

The living cell is the most complex system known to man. Its host of specialised molecules, many found nowhere else but within living material, are themselves enormously complex. They execute a dance of exquisite fidelity, orchestrated with breath-taking precision. Vastly more complicated than the most complicated ballet, the dance of life encompasses countless molecular performers in synergetic coordination.

Let us briefly look at some of this complexity, remembering that this is where life began.

The bacteria membrane[30]

Too often, it is assumed that the first cells began with a simple, soap-bubble-type membrane. This simply would not work. The membrane surrounding a bacterium carries out numerous essential functions, including the controlled transport of water-soluble substances in and out of the cell. The membrane consists of two layers of lipids, spanned by over 50 different proteins. Transport of ions across the membrane is achieved using specialised proteins that interact with the ion molecules on the outside, bind them at the surface of the membrane, change shape

---

[29] Davies, Paul. (1988). The Fifth Miracle. Allen Lane: Penguin
[30] See: Wolfe, Stephen L. (1993). Molecular and Cellular Biology. Brooks Cole

after the use of specialised enzymes, and then somehow 'squeeze' the ion molecules through the membrane into the internal cytoplasm.

The membrane also contains proteins that act as receptors by recognising and binding specific molecules that penetrate through the membrane from the surrounding medium. Binding these external molecules triggers internal reactions that allow the bacteria to sense and respond to their environment.

Of course, the construction of the membrane is coded by the DNA within the bacterium. Without the membrane, the DNA could not function; without the DNA, the membrane could not be made. Both are necessary from the beginning. This is one of the many *irreducibly complex* systems that we find in biology—I will devote a chapter on what irreducible complexity means later.

Darwin, through no fault of his own, knew nothing of molecular biology and did not speculate about the origin of life, apart from thinking it might have formed in *"some warm little pond"*[31]. Theories abound, but no one has produced life in a laboratory nor has anyone, despite great efforts, given an answer to the problems I will outline here.

DNA

DNA is the extraordinary molecule found in every form of life. It serves as the blueprint for how each organism

---

[31] Darwin, Charles (1871). Letter to Joseph Hooker.

is constructed and functions. A bacterium such as *E. coli*, has millions of pieces of information encoded in its DNA. DNA orchestrates and codes for the making of proteins, which are the basic building blocks and engines of life. The process of making just one protein is incredibly complex and involves RNA, enzymes, ribosomes, and many other molecules. It is one of the most intricate and amazing processes known. All life has this ability.

No one has succeeded in synthesising DNA from scratch in a laboratory. Some of the building blocks, such as purines, do occur naturally. But for the formation of nucleic acids, the fundamental units of DNA, there are too many highly unlikely steps for this to have happened accidentally. Moreover, the formation of DNA would require a plethora of proteins, all of which would need to be coded for by the DNA itself. In other words, the entire system had to be in place from the beginning—another example of irreducible complexity.

One of the major problems with some form of accidental origin-of-life scenario is that when DNA is copied during cell division a sophisticated proofreading and error-correction mechanism must be in place. Without this, errors would quickly accumulate, leading to a catastrophic failure in genome copying. This process is performed by a suite of enzymes, which are proteins that can only be produced if DNA already exists. Only unacceptably short DNA sequences could survive without proof-reading and error correction.

Paul Davies once again points out the problem with the standard materialistic explanation:

A short nucleic acid sequence, as envisaged by evolutionists, would have no chance of containing the information needed to code for the copying enzymes that it needs. Complex genomes require reliable copying, and reliable copying requires complex genomes. Which came first?[32]

The Miller-Urey experiment to mimic creation of life in laboratory

In 1952, Miller and Urey conducted an experiment simulating conditions on the early earth by passing an electric arc (similar to lightning) through a flask containing methane, ammonia and hydrogen (simulating the early earth's atmosphere). This process produced some of the amino acids found in living cells and was hailed as a major breakthrough in understanding life's origin. It is still frequently cited in many biology textbooks. However, the atmosphere they used was incorrect. Moreover, the production of basic amino acids alone does not remotely explain how proteins could be assembled from them.

James Tour, a leading chemist specialising in origin-of-life research with over 830 publications and a Professor of Chemistry, Materials Science and Nanoengineering at Rice University, Texas, believes that only an intelligent creator could have made life.

---

[32] Davies, Paul (1998). The Fifth Miracle. Allen Lane: Penguin.

James Tour stated in an interview that since the Miller-Urey experiment in 1952, we have discovered that the cell is far more complex than we thought and *"goalposts have moved considerably further away"* from formulating any sort of pathway to the first cell.

The message in the molecules

DNA has meaningful information. There are two types of information, which computer scientists describe: syntactic and semantic. Syntactic information is like that in a snowflake. There is complex information there, but it is not meaningful—it does not carry a message or instructions.

The DNA molecule carries millions of *meaningful* instructions. This is semantic information, much like the software in a computer. In fact, there is no known physical system in the universe that carries semantic information without being designed. In other words, the codes in DNA cannot have arisen accidentally, as materialists suggest. The first DNA must have had these codes already in place from the start—intentionally.

It is worth quoting James Tour here:

> *We have no idea how the molecules that compose living systems could have been devised such that they would work in concert to fulfil biology's functions. We have no idea how the basic set of molecules, carbohydrates, nucleic acids, lipids and proteins were made and how they could have coupled in proper sequences, and then transformed into the ordered assemblies until there was the construction of a complex biological system, and eventually to*

that first cell. Those that say they understand are generally wholly uninformed regarding chemical synthesis...neither I nor any of my colleagues can fathom a prebiotic molecular route to construction of a complex biological system...I have asked all of my colleagues—National Academy members, Nobel Prize winners—I sit with them in offices. Nobody understands this.[33]

The more we understand about the simplest cell, the more we reason that a naturalistic origin of life is unobtainable.

And as philosopher Thomas Nagel writes: "*The more details we learn about the chemical basis of life and the intricacy of the genetic code, the more unbelievable the standard historical account becomes.*"[34]

It is worth listening to an episode of "In Our Time" on BBC Radio titled "The Habitability of Planets," recorded in December 2024 and available as a podcast. In this discussion, three world-class researchers specializing in the origins of life explain the latest developments. They include an Associate Professor of Exoplanetary Science at the University of Oxford, an Assistant Professor of Chemistry at King's College London, and a Professor of Natural Philosophy at the University of Cambridge. While they assume that a natural solution may one day be found, it is clear that,

---

[33] Quoted in Leisola, Matti and Witt, Jonathan. (2018). Heretic: One Scientist's Journey from Darwin to Design Discovery Institute.

[34] Quoted in Leisola, Matti and Witt, Jonathan. (2018). Heretic: One Scientist's Journey from Darwin to Design Discovery Institute.

despite great efforts, there is currently no plausible explanation for how chemicals on the early Earth came together to form the first life.

CHAPTER 4

AN EXPLOSION OF LIFE

Darwinian evolution has certain very key rules. One of these is that there can only be very gradual small increments of change for evolution to occur. This is because the mechanism for change, mutations in DNA, are accidental, undesigned mistakes (mutations) in the genetic code. Only small changes can occur at a time because errors in DNA sequencing cannot produce entirely new body plans simultaneously. Achieving a significant change would require impossibly rare and enormous re-arrangements in DNA sequencing. Most DNA coding errors are harmful or have negligible effects.

Research has found that there are severe limitations on what mutations can accomplish.[35] [36] Therefore, when the fossil record reveals brand new biological forms, without transitional ancestors, we must question the entire edifice built around evolutionary theory.

The Cambrian explosion is one such fatal test of the Darwinian paradigm.

The Cambrian Explosion

Fossils are wonderful things. I personally love seeing and handling them. They provide a window into the past, almost transporting us to realms millions and even billions of years ago.

Darwin was very knowledgeable about the fossils discovered in his time. It was partly his study of ancient forms in the fossil record that encouraged him in 1859 to publish his ground-breaking work, *The Origin of Species*[37]. One observation that caused him some concerns was the apparently sudden appearance of highly advanced animals around 530 million years ago, during the Cambrian period of geological history (then known as the Silurian period). He wrote:

---

[35] See Behe, Michael (2007). The Edge of Evolution. Free Press.
[36] Axe, Douglas (2010). The case against a Darwinian origin of protein folds Bio-complexity. Vol, 2010.
[37] Darwin, Charles (1985). On the Origin of Species. Penguin books.

"The case at present remains inexplicable, and may be truly urged as a valid argument against the views here entertained."[38]

Darwin attributed this to the incompleteness of the fossil record. He believed that future discoveries would reveal many fossils found in the lower strata, showing gradual evolution. Today, however, we have a worldwide record of the geology and palaeontology of that era, and his prediction has been found to be spectacularly false.

As we have seen, the first organisms we know from the rocks were bacteria and were found from roughly 3.46 billion years ago. Known also as prokaryotes bacteria, though containing DNA, do not have a nucleus. Larger cells with a nucleus, known as eukaryote cells, appeared around 2.8 billion years ago. All animal bodies have eukaryote cells. For a long period, only these two types of single-celled organisms existed on earth.

There was a dramatic and extraordinary appearance of multicellular life about 530 million years ago, widely known as the *Cambrian explosion*. During this period, a diverse array of complex sea-dwelling creatures appeared in the geological strata.[39] They include animals with eyes, nervous systems, intestines, digestive glands, sensory organs, bristles and very complex and

---

[38] Darwin, Charles (1985). On the Origin of Species. Penguin books, p.313

[39] For a superb introduction to the Cambrian explosion see: Gould, S.J. (2000). Wonderful Life Vintage

developed body types. Even 'died in the wool' Darwinists call this an explosion. It is undeniable.

Opabinia: one of the strange Cambrian animals

All life is classified into basic body plans known as phyla. The extraordinary fact is that at least half of (and many palaeontologists think up to three-quarters), of today's 40 phyla appeared suddenly and dramatically in a very short period of time during the Cambrian explosion, which lasted a mere 5-10 million years. These include all the invertebrate phyla. Moreover, many other animal phyla appeared alongside the known ones. These body plans include the arthropods, molluscs, echinoderms and our own phylum—the chordates. This is called 'disparity': a wide range of entirely separate forms with no obvious links between them.

The period just before the Cambrian is known as the Vendian. There are a few multicellular fossils seen in what is called the Vendian biota, including sponges and other ill-defined fossils. Apart from possibly some molluscs, none of these fossils show any discernible links to the Cambrian animals. Unlike Darwin's time, we do have a very clear understanding of the fossil data before and during the Cambrian explosion.

The first Cambrian fossils were found in the Burgess Shale of Canada in the early 20th century, and similar findings have since been confirmed in geological strata throughout the world, particularly in Chengjian, China. The few forms known to have existed just before the Cambrian do not support the gradual evolutionary transitions expected by Darwinian Theory.

What amazes us most is the rich complexity of forms. We see here the first fully developed compound eyes appearing suddenly, as in the trilobites. Compound eyes have no advantage unless they are fully and magnificently constructed with intact nervous systems in place. Every facet of the eye must be orientated and focused and the image connected to its nervous system. These were magnificently advanced creatures. Such a dramatic appearance of eyes cannot be explained by random genetic mutations.

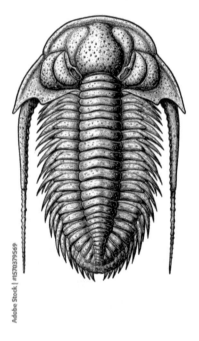

Fossil Trilobite

Given the complexity and beauty of the fauna we see in the Cambrian, it is worth contemplating again what this means on the level of DNA. Even a tiny worm (e.g. *Caenorhabditis elegans*) has 97 million base pairs in its DNA genome. These are the units of the DNA molecule which code information. Although the number of base pairs in insects varies enormously, bees have one of the smaller genomes, with approximately 300 million base pairs. These Cambrian animals must have possessed very large genomes, and there is currently no theoretical model to account for such an amount of specified information without intelligent input.

Molecular biologist Douglas Axe has determined the odds of random mutations producing the right sequence of base pairs in DNA required to form even a single functional protein domain[40]. It is 1 in $10.^{77}$ These odds simply rule out any random process in producing the rich fauna of the Cambrian explosion.

In his book, *On the Origin of Species*, Darwin illustrated his concept of gradually evolving life. It is in the form of a tree with a single trunk at its base, branching over time into many distinct forms. The Cambrian explosion totally refutes this picture. Rather than a tree with one trunk, there are multiple beginnings at a point in time, each phylum developing on its own from a wide base, but firmly remaining as a distinct body plan.

The Cambrian explosion overturns the foundation of Darwinism; the gradual incremental change that is essential for the theory.

As we follow the phyla in the fossil record over millions of years up to the present, we observe change; however, every significant new development occurs suddenly. This brings us to the next subject: microevolution and macroevolution.

---

[40] Axe, Douglas (2004). Estimating the Prevalence of Protein Sequences Adopting Functioning Enzyme Folds. Journal of Molecular Biology. p. 3415

CHAPTER 5

MICROEVOLUTION AND MACROEVOLUTION

When I was at school, I learned all the basics of evolutionary theory in our excellent biology class. My children learned the same—with little changes in content, and current textbooks have not been altered significantly. I became friendly with our children's biology teacher and there seemed no obvious deviation from the standard line taught 60 years ago.

Two of the most impressive pieces of evidence supporting the theory concerned, firstly, the Galapagos finches (also known as Darwin's finches), and the secondly, the peppered moth. If you have studied biology, these will stir memories.

When Darwin visited the Galapagos Island, as an astute observer (and he was one of the best), he observed the variation in the finches that inhabited the various islands.[41] At that time, he had not formulated any clear evolutionary theory but brought some specimens to England. It was actually the ornithologist, John Gould, who analysed the specimens and drew Darwin's attention again to the variations.

What is clear is that the finches seem to be from ancestral species that lived on mainland America. The very interesting thing is that, on each island, the finches seem to have evolved according to the particular food sources available. This is seen particularly in the beaks, some best for seeds, and some best for cracking nuts. Each isolated island has finches with beaks adapted to the particular food available.

This is still held up as evolution in action, as if it accounts for what happens over millions of years to produce the variety of animals on earth today.

I also learnt about the peppered moth (sometimes known as Kettlewell's moth). During the industrial revolution in England, the pollution in the air caused

---

[41] Darwin, Charles (1986). Journal of the Beagle. William Pickering. Vol 2. p. 461

the bark of trees in cities to become black. What was observed was that these moth species seemed to adapt to this by changing to a dark-winged form from its normal lichen coloured form. This allowed it to be camouflaged from predating birds. In areas where there was no pollution, the lichen coloured one predominated.

This is still held up as evolution in action—a great example to support Darwin's theory. As a teenager, I was impressed by this evidence.

What is actually happening in these cases? We need to understand that there are always variations within any population of organisms. Within the genome of the species, there is an opportunity for natural selection to work on these variations. Each individual is different genetically. The genetics of this is actually fairly simple—if you isolate two groups of finches on different islands with different food sources, you will inevitably get selection of the most useful beaks from the available variability within the gene pool. This accounts for the different finches. Note: This does not create any new genetic information at all; it simply involves the selection of certain existing genes. Although the different finches are known as different species, there is good evidence that if you change the food source on an island, you can even see reversion to the original type. There is also evidence of interbreeding between the different species. There is even doubt that they are separate species at all.[42]

All this is even more evident in the case of peppered moths. Before the industrial revolution, there were dark forms, even if less common than the lichen-coloured ones. All that happened was a temporary selection from the existing dark form. Notice that this does not involve any new genetic information.

Sometimes, a mutation may alter the genetic makeup of an individual and, if this is advantageous, it may be selected to continue. However, mutations in organisms have never been shown to do more than tinker with what is already there. There are limitations to what mutations can do—they might alter a colour or lengthen a limb, but nothing *substantially* new occurs. Mutations never account for the big changes—for example, the Cambrian animals, wings, or human brains.

Michael Behe, the biochemist, has clearly demonstrated this in his book 'The Edge of Evolution'.[43] He has painstakingly researched the evidence, particularly from micro-organisms. Micro-organisms have such a rapid generation time that observing their evolution is like seeing the whole of human history in a few years. The evidence is clear—mutations confer very minimally advantageous changes to the genome. The big steps in life's history are certainly not to the result

---

[42] McKay B. D. and Zink R. M. (2014). Sisyphean evolution in Darwin's finches. Biological review. 90 (3) pp. 689-698

[43] Behe, Michael (2007). The Edge of Evolution. Free Press.

of random mistakes; on the contrary, they have all the hallmarks of design.

We all know about the 'evolution' of bacteria when they become resistant to antibiotics. Behe and others have shown that such 'evolution' does not confer some brand-new useful process or structure, rather it is the breaking or altering of existing molecular functions that confers such resistance (as in alteration of the cell surface binding sites).[44]

Thus, microevolution occurs, but it primarily involves the selection of existing genetic material or, more rarely, very small changes due to mutations. *Macroevolution, however,* is something altogether different-it is what we observe when new body plans appear.[45]

Personally, I feel that young people in schools are being short-changed, as I was. If the evidence does not remotely support Darwinian evolution, why is it still being taught as if it does?

Human Brain

What is inside your head-the human brain- is the most complex object known in the universe. It is three times the size of our nearest ape 'relative', the chimpanzee,

---

[44] Abebe, E., et al. (2016) A review on molecular mechanisms of bacterial resistance to antibiotics. European Journal of Applied Sciences. Vol. 8 (5): 301-310

[45] See for example the continued perplexity about this problem in: Rolland J. et al. (2023). Conceptual and empirical bridges between microevolution and macroevolution Nature Ecology and evolution. Vol. 7, pp. 1181-1193

and three times larger than that of our assumed ancestor from just 3 million years ago, *Australopithecus afarensis.*[46] When I say "a *mere* 3 million years ago," I do so carefully. It is a tiny fraction of earth's history of life. Moreover, due to humans' long generation times and relatively small numbers of offspring, there has been very limited opportunity for mutations to produce the enormous changes observed in the human cortex.[47] Human cognition and language are not simply due a scaling up in size; they are due to profound structural changes coded for in new genetic instructions. In fact, there are at least 16 million *'fixed genetic changes'* for brain development that distinguish us any putative ape ancestor.[48] The human brain can only have appeared by macro evolution—and as we have seen, this cannot be explained by any known naturalistic route. It is hard to see how anyone who knows a little about the brain could imagine it being constructed by random mistakes—no matter how long that took.

---

[46] Kimbel W. H. and Delezene L. K. (2009). "Lucy" redu review of research on Australopithecus afarensis. American Journal of Biological Anthropology. 140 (S49), pp. 2-48

[47] Enard, W. (2016). The Molecular Basis of Human Brain Evolution. Current Biology, 26 (20). pp. 1109-1117

[48] Enard, W. (2016). The Molecular Basis of Human Brain Evolution. Current Biology, 26 (20) pp. 1109-1117

Common descent?

One of the big questions is whether there is actually common descent in the history of life. For example, did land animals descend from sea-dwelling creatures? Or did humans descend from apes?

My own view, looking at the fossil evidence, is that common descent is an open question. It is the *mechanism* of change that is in dispute. Darwinian Theory asks us to believe that all the changes were essentially random mutations acted upon by natural selection. So far, I hope that I have convinced you that this is quite impossible. Only specified information, by design, can account for what we see.

Homology

Homology refers to the similarity between structures in different species due to a shared ancestry. The classic case is that of the forelimbs of vertebrates. There is a common pattern of bones in humans, bats, birds and even the front flippers of whales.

Darwin was convinced that this showed a common evolutionary ancestry for all vertebrates. There are at least two reasons to question this.

Firstly, homology cannot be used as evidence for evolution because it assumes the very thing it's trying to prove. In fact, it is a circular way of thinking. There are two possible reasons for finding similar structures in different species: design or evolutionary common descent (through natural selection acting on random mutations). The argument for design is simple and can be illustrated looking at human-made designs. For example, consider a Model T Ford car and a modern Ford car. Both have four wheels, combustion engines and steering wheels. However, we would never say that the modern car is directly and physically descended from the Model T. The similarities between them are due to design—a common design concept. In the same way, the similarity of the forelimbs of different vertebrates could be due to common design rather than common descent. Insisting that homology is due to evolution is simply asserting an opinion, not presenting verifiable facts.

Secondly, we *should* observe shared early embryological development of structures that are considered homologous. I quote from David Swift here:

Structures and organs in a mature organism arise and develop...through the operation of formative processes as the embryo grows and develops. These embryological developmental processes operate consistently, such that it is possible to identify which cells in a very early embryo will develop into specific structures of the mature organism.

It has long been accepted, including by evolutionists that the early stages of embryological development will not be susceptible to change because later development depends on it and changes to early development will lead to detrimental deformities rather than something useful.[49]

A classic example of homology is the vertebral column seen in all vertebrates. In fact, contrary to Darwinian evolution theory, we see in the embryo completely different ways of forming the vertebrae using different lines of tissue between tetrapods (reptiles, birds, and mammals), cartilaginous fish (e.g. Shark) and Teleosts (most fish). A standard text on this subject (Kardong, 2009). *Vertebrates: comparative anatomy, function, and evolution*[50], confirms the finding.

And so, homology is by no means a pillar in the Darwinian edifice.

Microevolution and macroevolution are different concepts. The former is well described and understood. The latter is not—and speaks of design.

---

[49] UK Centre for Intelligent Design: Homology - Evidence for or against evolution?

[50] Kardong (2009). Vertebrates: comparative anatomy, function, and evolution. Chapter 8: Skeletal system: The axial skeleton. McGraw-Hill.

CHAPTER 6

IRREDUCIBLE COMPLEXITY

As we have seen so far, Darwinian evolution requires gradual small changes to have occurred. Anything more than this would be considered statistically impossible—no mutation could form a completed new structure with a new function. We have seen that even the production of one protein is so unlikely that it would take 10^{77} attempts at finding the right combination of base pairs on DNA[51]. That is about the number of particles in the universe.

Darwin wrote very honestly in *The Origin of Species*:

> *"If it could be demonstrated that any complex organ existed, which could not possibly have been formed by numerous, successive slight modifications, my theory would absolutely break down".*[52]

What if we find structures in living organisms that have to be fully developed *before* they can confer any evolutionary advantage? In other words, what if there are no beneficial steps in evolution that could lead from a simple form to the final product? If this were the case, then Darwinian evolution is simply out-ruled. This is known as irreducible complexity—complexity that cannot be arrived at by slow, gradual steps.

The bacterial flagellum

The term "irreducible complexity" was coined by Michael Behe in his ground-breaking book, *Darwin's Black Box*.[53] Probably the most iconic example, out of many, is that of the bacterial flagellum.

---

[51] Axe, Douglas. (2004). Estimating the Prevalence of Protein Sequences: Adopting Functioning Enzyme Folds. Journal of Molecular Biology, 341:5

[52] Darwin, Charles. (1859). The Origin of Species. New York: Bantam Books.

[53] Behe, M. (1996). Darwin's Black Box: the biochemical challenge to evolution. New York: The Free Press.

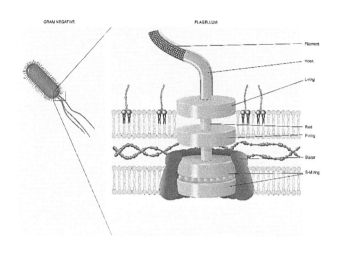

Bacterial flagellum

The flagellum of bacteria is a remarkable machine that is made of about 30 different proteins. It is basically a form of rotary motor that the bacteria use for movement. Just like an artificial motor, the bacterial flagellum consists of a rotor, stator, drive shaft, universal joint, bushing, bearings and a whip-like filament. It can rotate at speeds to 100,000 RPM and can even reverse direction. The flagellum is connected to a sensory system that detects food gradients in its environment, allowing the bacterium to move toward nutrients. The sensory system also signals it to move away from repellent chemicals. As you can imagine, constructing such a complex machine requires highly specified genes. Beneficial functions must exist at every stage of its evolution because there can be no half-finished flagellum—it either works or it does not.

Moreover, the flagellum is useless without the sensory and signalling systems that guide the bacterium's movement.

Michael Behe cited the flagellum as one of many examples of irreducible complexity, arguing that the evolutionary process could not have produced it gradually. Was he right?

Of course, those who champion neo-Darwinism have come out with their defence, involving another piece of bacterial apparatus called the type III secretary system (type III SS). This system secretes proteins from inside the cell and closely resembles the base of the flagellar motor. It also plays a role in flagellum assembly. The argument is that the type III SS evolved first, and the flagellum either derived from it or from a common ancestor shared by both systems. This hypothesis offers a possible stepwise evolutionary pathway for the flagellum, providing some support to Darwinian explanations of its origin.

Why does this not work for the Darwinist? Firstly, we know that the genes to form a flagellum are in fact older than those for the type III SS. When examining groups of genes, we can detect what is called 'mutational density', which is a measure of accumulated mutations over time. Higher mutational density indicates older gene groups. The mutational density in flagellar genes exceeds that of genes coding for the type 111 SS, indicating that the flagellum likely originated first. Also, we know that the distribution of flagella in multiple types of bacteria is very wide, whereas the Type III SS is restricted to a much smaller range of Gram-negative ones. This widespread prevalence further supports the flagellum being older and rules out the Type III SS being part of its evolution.

Secondly, the Darwinian explanation for the evolution of the Type III SS to a flagellum does not make sense. In Darwinism, every single step on the way to the flagellum must confer a survival advantage and be selected. The mutations responsible for this are entirely blind and random. There are no theoretical or conceivable steps to the flagellar motor from the Type III SS.

I believe the iconic bacterial flagellum stands firmly as a counter to evolution by random mutations. Some decades have passed since Behe demonstrated this and there has been no reasonable argument to oppose his view—it is irreducibly complex.

When I discussed the bacterial cell, I also provided several examples of irreducible complexity—most notably the cell membrane, the structure of DNA, and the necessity of proof-reading enzymes from the very beginning to ensure accurate replication. In fact, each of our cells contain a host of sophisticated nano-machines performing extraordinary functions. I recommend looking at this short YouTube video, *The Nano Robots inside you*, from the World Science Festival in 2014, to get a sense of this.[54]

---

[54]https://www.youtube.com/results?search_query=the+nano+ro bots+inside+you

The eye

Life is crammed full of irreducible complexity. I will now look at the human eye as another example.

Charles Darwin once wrote to a friend very honestly: *"The eye to this day gives me a cold shudder"*. He also wrote: *"To suppose that the eye with all its inimitable contrivances for adjusting the focus to different distances, for admitting different amounts of light, and for the correction of spherical and chromatic aberration, could have been formed by natural selection, seems, I confess, absurd in the highest degree"*.

There have been many attempts by evolutionists to explain how such an intricate and complex organ could have come about through natural selection acting on random mutations. The most famous is Richard Dawkins. In his book, 'The Blind Watchmaker' he tries to explain this process by posing two questions:

1. *Could the human eye have arisen directly from no eye at all, in a single step?*

2. *Could the human eye have arisen directly from something slightly different from itself, something that we may call X?*[55]

He, of course, dismisses the first question and answers yes to the second. His reasoning is as follows: if X is something very nearly like a human eye, then the human eye could plausibly have arisen from X through a tiny alteration. If we accept this, then we can accept

---

[55] Dawkins, R. (1986). The Blind Watchmaker Longman Scientific and Technical. Pp. 77

that X itself could have arisen from a more primitive, fractionally different X...and so on. Using this line of reasoning, he argues that the eye could indeed have arisen through small incremental changes without any design. I quote:

My feeling is that, provided the difference between neighbouring intermediaries in our series leading to the eye is sufficiently small, the necessary mutations are almost bound to be forthcoming. We are after all, talking about minor quantitative changes in an existing embryonic process.[56]

Dawkins is giving us unsubstantiated 'feelings' here. He claims that the only changes required are *'quantitative'* changes in what already exists. If this is what he believes, then he must also believe that the most primitive, original eye had no *qualitative* difference from a modern eye. In other words, it must have had a capsule, eye muscles, cornea, iris, lens, retina (including the molecular machinery to convert photons to meaningful electric signals) and a nervous system to interpret it all. These are the most obvious qualities of the human eye. He is trying to convince us and himself that the mutations required are simply a little bit more or a little bit less of what is already there (quantitative changes).

Of course, this is nonsense. To develop an eye in the Darwinian sense, there must have been countless genetic changes to give entirely new, *qualitatively* different characteristics. Take the iris, for instance. It

[56] Dawkins, R. (1986). The Blind Watchmaker Longman Scientific and Technical. Pp. 79

must have arisen somehow *de novo* and acquired, from the start, many new, complex characteristics such as its position in front of the lens, its shape and ability to open and close, and its nervous system connections that intricately adjust the aperture in response to varying light and for accommodation (when we look at something near, the pupil gets smaller). These are major *new* characteristics and not mere modifications of what already existed. Therefore, to claim that it is possible to imagine a long series of Xs with almost undetectable differences in smooth transition with almost undetectable differences between successive stages is preposterously wrong.

Let us look at just one remarkable structure of the eye—the superior oblique muscle.

Muscles of the Human Eye

superior oblique
(downward and outward movement)

superior rectus
(upward movement)

lateral rectus
(outward movement)

medial rectus
(inward movement)

inferior rectus
(downward movement)

inferior oblique
(upward and outward movement)

The Superior Oblique muscle

The superior oblique muscle is one of the six external muscles in each eye. It has a fascinating and unique anatomy. Arising from an attachment in the bony orbit, its tendon goes forward and passes through a loop attached to the orbit called the trochlea. After looping through the trochlea, the tendon doubles back and inserts onto the top of the eye. When it contracts, it moves the eye downward and tends to rotate it inward. Functionally, it always acts in opposition to the inferior oblique muscle, which lies under the eye and moves the eye in an equal and opposite direction. Neither muscle can act without being in tension with the other. The superior oblique muscle, like all the other eye muscles must act in harmony and in tandem with the other five external muscles of each eye.

The control of eye movements is not fully understood and is immensely complex. Even when you fix your gaze on an object, your eyes must have slight, shivering movements so that the image on the retina is not stationary. If stationary, then the image will rapidly fade.

As an illustration, while reading this, try bending your head towards one shoulder. Your eyes will compensate for this movement so that your gaze remains steady on what you are looking at. This is primarily done by a reflex nervous connection between the vestibular canals in your inner ear, which detect the head movement, and the eye muscles. All the eye muscles must work together to achieve this. You are unconscious of this process, and it is a wonderful and still poorly understood mechanism.

The image you see is a composite of the input from both eyes. Any defect of the external eye muscles will cause double vision. To achieve a single image, particularly for close objects, it requires a binocular coordination of the eyes; the eyes are positioned at slightly different angles to achieve a single image.

Why is this important for discussing intelligent design? It is important because there is no evolutionary mechanism to produce a muscle like the superior oblique. The muscle is irreducibly complex and there are no known intermediate steps in evolutionary terms. Much of what I have written could apply just as well to the other parts of the eye.

Firstly, look at its anatomy. The minimum requirements for it to work at all is that it must loop through the trochlea and back on itself to attach to the eye-ball. It must have a minimum of a bony attachment in the orbit, a trochlea to pass through, an insertion into the top of the eyeball, an intimate connection to the nervous system, and a blood supply. Its attachments must be precisely positioned to have any use. Without the trochlea, it would not work. All must be in place perfectly for it to function.

Consider how the superior oblique muscle must work in harmony with the other muscles of the eye. It maintains dynamic tension with the inferior oblique muscle and must be connected through the nervous system to various centres that coordinate its function with the other eye muscles. There is the vestibular apparatus, which we have mentioned, as well as the unconscious micro movements that allow you fix your gaze on one object, the binocular coordination required for focusing on close objects and, of course, the action of voluntarily moving your gaze.[57]

As repeatedly emphasised, for the Darwinist, there must be a possible series of intermediate steps all leading to something as complex as the superior oblique muscle. No evolutionary thinker would think it could arise de novo, as it is now. The first step must be simple and only require some mutation to create a novel structure. Then each subsequent step must have an improvement or survival value for it to be selected and passed on to future generations.

The problem is that the superior oblique is not only complex but also requires a minimum set of specific attributes to function at all—those that I have listed. The removal of any of these may result in a complete and total breakdown of vision.

Eyes of various types have evolved many times in the animal kingdom. The 'camera' eye type, which we possess, has developed independently many times. There is no smooth trajectory from simple to complex eyes in the fossil record[58] or as propounded by Richard Dawkins.

---

[57] Oyster, Clyde. (1999). The Human Eye. Structure and Function. Sinauer.
[58] Land & Nilsson (2002). Animal Eyes. Oxford.

The very first eyes, which we find in the lower Cambrian strata, about 530 million years ago are superb compound eyes seen on the trilobite.[59] They appear abruptly and are magnificently engineered. And when vertebrate eyes appear in the fossils, they do so abruptly also.

Life is replete with irreducible complexity.

[59] Clarkson, E.N.K. (1998). Invertebrate Palaeontology & Evolution. Blackwell.

CHAPTER 7

DARWIN THE MAN

No scientist is uninfluenced by the prevailing beliefs and philosophies of the time he or she lives in. Darwin, though a systematic observer, was clearly influenced by many ideas which were current when he lived. It is therefore a useful exercise to examine some of these when making a critique of Darwin as well as looking at traits in his character which may have led him to his theory.

Darwin's evolutionary influences

I believe that it is no coincidence that one of the most influential and talked about authors on evolution during Darwin's early years was his own grandfather Erasmus Darwin. As a teenager, Darwin read *Zoonomia*[60] his grandfather's best-known work, written between 1794 and 1796. In this work, Erasmus Darwin postulated a theory very similar to the type of evolution proposed by Jean-Baptiste Lamarck, which involves the inheritance of *acquired* characteristics. In Charles Darwin's own brief autobiography, he reflects on his time as a medical student in Edinburgh and states:

I had previously read the 'Zoonomia' of my grandfather in which similar views are maintained, but without producing any effect on me. Nevertheless, it is probable that the hearing rather early in life such views maintained and praised may have favoured my upholding of them under a different form in my 'Origin of Species'. At this time, I greatly admired 'Zoonomia' but on reading it a second time after an interval of 10 or 15 years, I was much disappointed; the proportion of speculation being so large to the facts given.[61]

Here we have evidence of his own admission that *Zoonomia* likely had an influence on him writing *The*

---

[60] Darwin, Erasmus (1794). Zoonomia. 2022 Edition. Legare Street Press.

[61] Darwin, C. (1888). The Life and Letters of Charles Darwin. Edited by F. Darwin, 2009 edition. Cambridge University Press, p. 38.

Origin of Species. Darwin later recognised how unscientific the speculations of his grandfather were. Nevertheless, it seems that during his most impressionable years, he revered this book and, at least subconsciously, absorbed much of its thrust.

During his period in Edinburgh, he spent much time with Robert Grant, a zoologist who was an expert on sponges. He became closer to Darwin and did more to influence him than anyone else in this period[62].

Robert Grant was sixteen years older than Charles Darwin and a doctor who had given up medical practice to study marine life. He was a free thinker, who believed that only physical and chemical forces were involved in life, rejecting any notion of a spiritual power behind the natural world. Grant was outspoken in his praise of Lamarckian evolution and held convictions very fervently. During Darwin's formative years, Grant was his walking companion. He was very anti-clerical and rejected the church's claims that the fossil record showed a series of divine creations. Grant was a very well-travelled man and a good raconteur, someone who kept the impressionable Darwin very much absorbed.

It would be wrong, however, to think that Darwin took all that Grant believed 'hook, line and sinker.' Later, after giving up medicine, he went to Cambridge to study to be a clergyman, and firmly believed every world of the Bible, learning Paley's *Evidences for Christianity* by heart. *Evidences* was the classic argument

---

[62] See Desmond, A. and Moore, J. (1991). Darwin Penguin.

for design used by many at the time to uphold creation. Nevertheless, one gets the impression that Darwin's understanding of Christian doctrine and his belief in it were somewhat superficial, and shaped more by those around him than by any deep spiritual revelation of his own.

There is little doubt that both his grandfather and Grant influenced Darwin when he was young and somewhat without direction, paving the way for his later convictions about the origins of life.

Having read many books about Darwin and his own autobiography, I get an impression of a sincere young man, an avid collector of beetles and fascinated by nature, who was nevertheless highly impressionable. He had performed poorly at school and was about to give up the idea of becoming a doctor. His father was disappointed in him and worried about his obsession with nothing but shooting game during his holidays.

Darwin courted the illustrious and learned men of the day in Edinburgh and later in Cambridge—almost as a compensation for his lack of success. Even in his autobiography, written when he was 67, he spends much of it recounting his meetings with the most famous scientists of the day—not very far from name-dropping. Probably more than most, he was greatly influenced by authoritative figures around him.

Darwin's ideas on evolution did not come out of a vacuum of pure objectivity (no one's ideas do of course). He himself confessed in his autobiography, with his characteristic modesty, that he was a poor critic of ideas when they first came to him. There is a sort of naivety in his acceptance of the thoughts of others. Here is a fascinating excerpt from that autobiography:

I have no great quickness of apprehension or wit which is so remarkable in some clever men, for instance Huxley. I am therefore a poor critic; a paper or book, when first read, generally excites my admiration, and it is only after considerable reflection that I perceive the weak points. My power to follow along a purely abstract train of thought is very limited; and therefore, I could never have succeeded in metaphysics or mathematics. My memory is extensive, yet hazy; it suffices to make me cautious by vaguely telling me that I have observed or read something opposed to the conclusion which I am drawing, or, on the other hand, in favour of it. After a time, I can generally recollect where to search for my authority. So poor in one sense is my memory that I have never been able to remember for more than a few days a single date or a line of poetry.[63]

Darwin then goes on to say that, because of this, some of his critics have said he was a good observer but had no power of reasoning. He refutes this by referring to *The Origin of Species* as *'one long argument from beginning to the end'*.[64] There is no doubt that the *Origin of Species* is a carefully argued book, honed over many years of preparation. But this does not mean that it was a purely objective piece of reasoning. Probably no scientific theory is.

---

[63] Darwin, C. (1888). The Life and Letters of Charles Darwin. F. Darwin (Ed.). 2009. Cambridge University Press, p.102
[64] Ibid.

However, it seems that, in the case of Darwin, there was much more in his background to influence his ideas than with most scientists. I would maintain that he already had strong inclinations toward evolutionary theories long before he fully developed his ideas after his voyage on the *Beagle,* and that these were strongly influenced by the essentially atheist philosophies of Erasmus Darwin and Robert Grant. This would explain why he latched on to facts to support the theory, such as the geographical distribution of species. We now know (or should know) that small changes in groups of organisms such as the Galapagos finches are not due to any new information in the genome but to the reshuffling of existing genetic material within a species—yet such small variations were a key foundation of *The Origin of Species*. Likewise, we now know that another foundation for his theory, artificial selection in domestic breeds, is not due to any significant new genetic information and cannot account for the macro changes in the fossil record.

He held on to these illusory foundations for his theory because he had already become convinced of his ideas. Even his 'bulldog' and champion, Huxley, baulked at extrapolating the findings of pigeon fanciers to claims about the evolution of, for example, the eye. Darwin, however, once his course was set, could not break away from the rigid rules of gradual, imperceptible change that he had established. He preferred to apply the findings of domestic breeders to support his theory rather than acknowledge its limitations and accept the alternative—saltationism (the sudden appearance of major new forms).

The ambitious Darwin

Darwin was in one sense, a humble man but, paradoxically, there is strong evidence that he was extremely ambitious and determined to make a name for himself in the world of science. It is worth looking at this aspect of his character because it influenced the way in which he saw his theory and the acclaim that it would bring. He did not know for sure that it would be celebrated and indeed it suffered much criticism; but in the end, he was at the top of the scientific establishment, the very thing he had dreamt of.

That he was very keen to make a name for himself comes through in his autobiography. When studying at Cambridge, he continued his childhood pastime of collecting beetles. One specimen was very rare, and his name was associated with its discovery. Describing his feelings in the autobiography, he wrote: *'No poet ever felt more delighted at seeing his first poem published than I did at seeing, in Stephens' Illustrations of British Insects, the magic words. 'Captured by C. Darwin, Esq.* [65]

Later in his autobiography, Darwin admits to being very ambitious and eager to gain notoriety amongst top scientists. While on the *Beagle,* he heard that his former Cambridge geology teacher, Sedgwick, had visited his father and said that *"I should take a place among the leading*

[65] Ibid. pp. 51-52

scientific men'[66] because of some scientific letters he had sent home that were published and also the fact that some fossil bones he had sent home had attracted considerable attention amongst the palaeontologists. He writes:

After reading this letter, I clambered over the mountains of Ascension with a bounding step, and made the volcanic rocks resound under my geological hammer. All this shows how ambitious I was; but I think that I can say with truth that in after years, though I cared in the highest degree for the approbation of such men as Lyle and Hooker, who were my friends. I did not care much about the general public.[67]

True, such ambition is common to many, but I feel that his need to be approved of by his father and the establishment was very great. We should remember that his mother died when he was only eight and he could remember nothing about her. His highly successful father dominated his early years and until the success of the research he had made on the Beagle, he had not shone at all. When a great theory about nature came to him, however gradually, it must have been intoxicating to think that he had solved the whole meaning of life's grandeur. While it is conjecture to imagine how this coloured his objectivity, it is worth our scrutiny.

---

[66] Ibid. pp. 66
[67] Ibid. pp.66

Darwin and geology

The principal influence on Darwin during the Beagle voyage was undoubtedly the work of Charles Lyell, the great geologist. Darwin brought with him the first volume of Lyell's great work, *Principles of Geology*, which had just been published. He read this avidly and was delighted to receive the second volume later in the voyage. Lyell's 'uniformitarian' approach to the history of the earth provided Darwin with a framework in which he could imagine the gradual process of evolution. Lyell painted a picture of a very ancient earth that had stayed unchanged over time (the opposite of catastrophism) with the sediments being laid down steadily over millions of years. This steady picture of the earth over long periods supported the idea of steady progression in the formation of new species. Lyell himself was not, at the time, an evolutionist. Although he remained a close friend of Darwin, he remained sceptical. Geologists now know that both catastrophism (volcanic activity, major climate changes, asteroidal impacts, etc.) and uniformitarianism are integral parts of the earth's history.

Therefore, the fact that Darwin was reading Lyell's work during the initial gestation of his theory has great significance. Had he known that the earth had regularly suffered catastrophes of climate and various impacts—with large scale extinctions—he would certainly have had less geological foundation for his work.

Darwin and naturalism

Every new scientific theory emerges within the context of the prevailing beliefs and philosophies of the time. These beliefs provide support both for the author of the theory and those who agree with it.[68]

Isaac Newton was, par excellence, the epitome of the great scientist and the model for how scientists in the nineteenth century should view the world. Darwin, along with much of society, was deeply influenced by 'Newtonianism'. In his species notebooks, he constantly followed the example of the major scientific philosophers of the time, Herschel and Whewell, by interpreting all science through the lens of invariable natural laws—as in Newtonian astronomy. Ironically, this was in spite of the fact that Newton himself believed in a God who could intervene in nature whenever he wished. At the end of 1838, Darwin reread the major works of Whewell (*History of the Inductive Sciences*) and Herschel (*A Preliminary Discourse on the Study of Natural Philosophy*). While neither were evolutionists, they admired and expounded the so-called Newtonian principles and the idea that science would eventually solve every mystery. When Darwin first read Herschel's *Discourse* at Cambridge he had been entranced. In his copy of the book, Darwin had written:

---

[68] See Ruse, M. (1999). The Darwinian Revolution. University of Chicago Press.

'To what then may we not look forward…what may we not expect from the exertions of powerful minds… 'building on the' …acquired knowledge of past generations?'

Darwin had also read with great interest a review of Comte's *Course de philosophie positive* which emphasised that all phenomena are subjected to invariable natural laws.

And so, there was a hubristic spirit that made him, and others think that everything in nature will one day be fully explained in a naturalistic manner.

The most influential philosopher in England at the time was John Stuart Mill, whose *System of Logic* was published in 1843[69]. He had enormous influence and was strongly in favour of absolute laws of nature and universal causation. He wrote: *"It is a law that every event depends on some law".*

This philosophic environment of inviolable laws and chains of causes influenced Darwin greatly. To Darwin, the appearance of life in all its forms must, like in Newton's astronomy, be under entirely natural laws that could be discovered and described. The idea of miracle was anathema to this way of thinking (and still is). Darwin wrote the following words to his friend Lyell on the subject of miracles:

"If I were convinced that I required such additions to the theory of Natural Selection, I would reject it as rubbish…I would give

---

[69] Mill, J. S. (1843) A system of Logic, Ratiocinative and Inductive 2011 Ed. Cambridge University Press.

nothing for the theory of Natural Selection if it requires miraculous additions at any one stage of descent.[70]

Darwin was therefore steeped in a prevailing naturalistic mind-set. Any idea of the supernatural was outrageous. It was on the arguably arrogant assumption that great men would one day describe all of nature and understand it that he wrote his great work *On the Origin of Species*.

Darwin and religion

It is important to realise the effect that German 'higher criticism' of the Bible was having, not just on the continent but also in England. As a result of this, there was a significant liberal branch of the church that questioned the authority of the Bible, and doubted anything miraculous. I have met members of the clergy who are exactly in this position today. Such liberalism was against any form of teleology (purpose) in the appearance of life. It therefore suited Darwinism well and certainly prepared the ground for it. Darwin was influenced by such theology and read such works as *Phases of Faith* by Francis Newman. This was at the time of his daughter Annie's terminal illness. Annie was a favourite and he was very close to her. In this book, Newman outlined an emotional, spiritual odyssey from orthodoxy to severe doubt. It echoed Darwin's own

---

[70] Darwin, C. (1888). The Life and Letters of Charles Darwin. Editor: F. Darwin 2009 ed. Cambridge University Press.

journey and he described the book as 'excellent' in his notebook. It is hard to know how much the subsequent tragic death of Annie affected his faith—and later, the bitter blow when Amy, the wife of his son Frank, died after childbirth. These painful experiences of loved ones dying did nothing to support any belief in a caring or benevolent creator.

In Victorian Britain, there was a great tension amongst thinkers and theologians between the traditional view of God as a benevolent gentleman figure who cared for every detail of his creation and the facts of biology such as the extinction of species, the apparent waste of life, and the bloody, seemingly heartless struggle for existence that lay behind the pastoral façade of nature. Darwin seems to have felt this very acutely and, throughout his writings, he continually refers back to this picture of a benevolent God who is incompatible with reality. According to Cornelius Hunter in his book *Darwin's God*[71], Darwin's theory of evolution was a form of theodicy—a way of accounting for evil by distancing God from his creation.

One of Darwin's favourite books was *Paradise Lost* by John Milton. He brought his copy of this on the voyage of the *Beagle*. The thrust of *Paradise Lost* is to solve the problem of evil with an emphasis on God letting humans choose between good and evil so that the good can be separated from the bad. Milton's God is pure but passive, distanced from the events of history.

---

[71] Hunter, C. (2001). Darwin's God. Brazos Press.

This view of God allowed one to see creation on its own terms, rather than under God's influence.

There is no evidence that Darwin lost faith in God completely, but it seems he accepted the idea that God is distant and uninvolved in nature.

In his autobiography, Darwin wrote about suffering and natural selection:

Suffering is quite compatible with the belief in Natural Selection, which is not perfect in its action, but tends only to render each species as successful as possible in the battle for life with other species, in wonderfully complex and changing circumstances.[72]

The background to Darwin's work involves a struggle to understand how God *ought* to behave. This was a constrained view of God that was prevalent in the nineteenth century. Even now, apologists for evolution constantly invoke God into their arguments. Richard Dawkins and others pepper their writings with concepts about how God *should* behave if He created us— particularly when speaking about suffering in nature. Hunter, in his book, argues that such a metaphysical foundation for doubting God is not actually science but rather a way of coping with one's own belief system. He writes:

From Milton to Leibniz, Hume, and others, modern intellectuals were rapidly moving away from the view that God

---

[72] Darwin, C. (1888). The Life and Letters of Charles Darwin. F. Darwin (Ed.). 2009 Edition. Cambridge University Press.

directly creates and controls the world, and towards the idea that God must be separated from evil. In the nineteenth century, these views played an important role in Darwin's development of evolution. The common denominator between Darwin's evolution and earlier theodicies is that God governs via secondary causes— his fixed natural laws—and that God is justified to humankind when we view natural evil as a result of some sort of cosmic constraint outside God. Darwin worked with this tradition, and it is no surprise that he arrived at his theory of evolution, which claims that nature's imperfections and evils arose from natural forces rather than a divine hand.[73]

Darwin, and many thinkers since have assumed that God is basically absent from his creation (a form of Deism), and this gave licence to pursue purely naturalistic explanations for all we see. For many, this has led to atheism. That this is a demonstrably false conclusion is why this book has been written.

Darwin's theory, therefore, like all others, was coloured by some degree of subjectivity and it is valid to critique it knowing this fact. There was his own grandfather's strong influence, Grant and his free-thinking atheism, Darwin's own personal powerful ambition, a prevailing nineteenth century philosophy of 'Newtonian' naturalism, and an emerging Victorian idea of what God should or should not do.

---

[73] Hunter, C. (2001). Darwin's God. Brazos Press.

CHAPTER 8

CONSCIOUSNESS AND THE SOUL

*H**ow could an idiotic universe have produced creatures whose mere dreams are so much stronger, better, subtler than itself? C.S. Lewis*

No one knows what consciousness is. It remains a deep mystery.

This may sound dogmatic, but having spent some years reading the literature on the subject and writing a book about it[74], I can say that neuroscientific research on consciousness has not shown any progress in decades. Philosophers continue to argue about it but come to no clear consensus. There are scores of philosophical theories about the nature of consciousness and whole university departments are devoted to the problem. How can something physical, such as the brain, be conscious? Philosopher of mind, David Chalmers, famously called it 'The Hard Problem'. The nature of consciousness has puzzled thinkers and scientists for millennia. How a material object can produce conscious thoughts, feelings, emotions, and intentions remains completely mysterious. Many philosophers and neuro-scientists have come to the conclusion that a proper theory of consciousness may forever be unattainable.

So let us examine some of the difficulties involved.

The definition of consciousness

Here, we immediately run into problems. Thomas Nagel famously wrote: *"There is something it is like to be conscious"*[75], which is about all we can say to get a grasp on it. We can describe our thoughts, sometimes wonderfully in great literature, but we are unable to pin down exactly what it is. Consciousness has been likened to the water a fish swims in; the fish does not think

---

[74] Latham, A. (2012). The Enigma of Consciousness: Reclaiming the Soul. Janus Publishing.

[75] Nagel, T. (1974). What is it like to be a bat? 2024 Ed. OUP: USA.

about being in water, just as most people do not wonder about the nature of consciousness. Perhaps by looking at some of the unique characteristics of consciousness, we can gain some insights—or perhaps not.

Consciousness is private

Your conscious thoughts are yours alone. Another way to say this is that you have privileged access to your thoughts or feelings. This is already extraordinary, as no physical object possesses such a privilege. A computer or robot may *appear* to be conscious, but I can examine its internal states and exactly describe what is happening to produce the illusion of consciousness. In contrast, our thoughts are entirely private and inaccessible to anyone else. And so, the following can be said:

1. Some mental states can only be privately accessed.

2. No physical state can be accessed privately.

3. Therefore, mental states are not physical states.[76]

You may ask whether one day, with more scientific knowledge, we could examine a person's brain and fully understand the nature of their thoughts. I will argue here, as many have done before, that because consciousness is not in fact a physical phenomenon, we will never be able to look at some neural network and decipher exactly what thoughts are occurring.

---

[76] Private communication from Peter S. Williams

Consciousness involves personhood

I know myself as an individual person and I recognise others as persons. While personhood may be hard to define, we intuitively know what it is. A person relates to other persons in a way that no machine can. You, as a person, exist over time and all your experiences shape you as a person while still being absolutely you. There is a richness and depth to personhood. Could a computer be a person – like HAL, depicted in the film 2001: *A Space Odyssey*? The answer is a clear no, and I will explain why later when discussing artificial intelligence.

Sensations

The simple sensation of seeing a colour like red is extraordinary. We do not merely register a certain wavelength (a computer or physical sensor could do that easily); we have an actual *experience* of redness. The same applies to the smell of coffee, the sound of the wind, or a pain in my foot. While we understand the neurological pathways and the physiology involved, can we know anything physical about the actual experience itself? Many philosophers argue that we cannot. Most even say that we will never have a physical description of a sensory experience. Sensory experiences and their phenomenal quality seem to belong to a completely different category than anything physical. It is rather like asking how heavy the number 7 is—it is simply a non-question.

There is a famous thought experiment known as Mary's room. In this thought experiment, Mary is the world's expert on the physiology, anatomy, and molecular intricacies of vision. Let's say she literally knows everything physical about vision, down to the last subatomic particle. However, Mary has grown up in a room that is only black and white and has never seen any colour, even though she knows all about how colour vision works. One day, she goes out of the room and sees the colour red for the first time. So, here are the crucial points:

- Mary knows all the physical facts about vision.

- Mary has experienced a new fact about vision.

- Therefore, not all facts about vision are physical.

The sensory experiences, known in philosophy as 'qualia', cannot be reduced to physical terms.

As Einstein once stated: *"Science cannot tell us the taste of chicken soup."*

Emotions

We all have emotions such as fear, sadness, love, and joy. These are deeply personal and very real. The issue then is: Can a physical object have emotions? A computer can mimic emotions (because someone programs it to) but does it experience an emotion, say sadness? Most philosophers and computer scientists would say no. Emotions, like sensations, are indefinable in physical terms.

Intentional thoughts

Intentional thoughts are thoughts *about* things. Examples include hopes and beliefs. A belief is always about something. For instance, I may have a belief that it will rain tomorrow. It is **about** something called rain. Right now, I am thinking about my wife. However, a physical system cannot be about anything. Neither a stone nor even a piece of complex tissue, such as a brain, can be about anything else.

You might argue that a piece of writing, for example, about the weight of Henry VIII, is about something. But the writing consists of symbols placed there by a conscious person. The marks on the page in themselves are not about anything—only the mind of someone reading them is. Therefore, the *aboutness* of intentional thought is something non-physical.

Consciousness has never been pinned down to any physical system. David Chalmers writes:

> *"There is something it is like to see a vivid green, to feel a sharp pain, to visualise the Eiffel Tower, to feel a deep regret, and to feel that one is late. Each of these states has a phenomenal character, with phenomenal qualities (or qualia) characterising what it is like to be in the state."[77]*

---

[77] Chalmers, D. (2003). Consciousness and its Place in Nature. The Blackwell Guide to Philosophy of Mind, Chapter 5.

There is, therefore, what is called the 'explanatory gap' between consciousness and brain activity. This gap represents the fundamental difficulty in explaining how physical processes in the brain give rise to subjective experiences or qualia. It is commonly regarded as the 'Hard Problem' in the philosophy of mind. It is fair to say that despite the efforts of some great minds, it has not been solved. It can be summarised as follows:

1. Physical accounts explain at most structure and function.

2. Explaining structure and function does not suffice to explain consciousness.

3. No physical account can explain consciousness.

The variety of philosophical 'isms' that try to explain consciousness

This is a quick tour of some of the ideas that attempt to explain what is happening in our minds:

Descartes 1596-1650

Descartes is considered to be the father of modern philosophy. In his famous work *Meditations*[78], he declared that there are two kinds of substances: Mind and Matter. These are distinct, yet they interact with and

---

[78]Descartes, R. (1641). Meditations in First Philosophy. 1985 edition. Cambridge University Press.

influence each other in both directions. According to Descartes, the mind cannot be divided, whereas matter can, including any part of the body. He said that the mind is not extended in space (i.e., does not have physical dimensions), unlike the body, which includes the brain.

He was therefore a dualist (a so-called Cartesian dualist, after his name). This view is also called substance dualism, which holds that there are 2 types of substance: mind and matter. In contrast, a monist believes there is only one substance – a physical one. Well-known philosophers who identify as substance dualists include Alvin Plantinga, Richard Swinburne, William Lane Craig, and J.P. Moreland.

It is important to emphasise that Descartes did not downplay the importance of the physical body. Rather, he argued that the mind is intimately linked with the body. Some Christians feel unhappy with the idea of an autonomous mind which is divorced somehow from the body. However, being a dualist does not require ignoring biology. Substance dualism can entail a complete, although contingent, unity between the mind and the body.

Since Descartes, many philosophers have attempted to challenge this idea of a non-material aspect of the mind. How could something non-material have any effect on the physical brain? This seems to contradict the laws of physics. The chapter on an 'open universe' tries to address this issue.

The great philosopher Leibniz also believed in a non-material mind. He imagined the brain as a machine, like a mill, and asked: how could the pieces or components of such a machine ever have perceptions, feelings, or thoughts?[79]

Let us go through some of the major ideas concerning the mind over the centuries:

Behaviourism: Mental events are nothing more than the observed behaviour. This view is out of fashion now. It says nothing about the internal mental states.

Type Identity theory: Mental events are nothing more than the physical biological processes. So, a pain **is** the firing of certain nerve fibres such as C fibres.

Firstly, this does not explain the phenomenon of our **experience** of pains or other sensations.

Secondly, we can imagine other species feeling pain who do not have the same C fibres.

Functionalism: Mental states are viewed as inputs and outputs from different brain states. Like a machine with parts that can be in different relationships. It is a monist view – only physical. There are many objections to this, including that it has nothing to do with intentional thoughts or experiences. It is very mechanical – where is consciousness in it?

---

[79] Leibniz G.W. '(1952). Monadology 17' in Philip Weiner (Ed.). Leibniz selections. Charles Scribners and sons.

Epiphenomenalism: This is a dualist position, but it differs from Descartes' view. It is a type of *property* dualism. According to this view, mental states are fundamentally different from physical states and are non-physical, yet are entirely produced by the brain. They are so-called 'supervenient' on the brain activity. However, mental states are considered inert; they cannot causally influence the brain.

However, this goes against all our experiences – it is the thoughts that initiate physical actions. I decide to move my arm by first thinking about it.

Eliminativism: In this radically reductionist view, mental states do not actually exist at all. All psychology is described purely in neuroscientific terms. One day, we will communicate simply by examining another person's brain. Eliminativism denies that our subjective experiences are real. Ideas we have about feelings and emotions are relegated to what is called 'folk psychology'.

Panpsychism

More recently, many modern philosophers have revived an ancient Greek idea that mind is a fundamental and widespread feature of nature. According to this view, some form of consciousness exists in all matter. It suggests that there is an unknown property inherent in all matter that is at least minimally conscious, which in humans develops into the most advanced form of consciousness.

This idea appeals to those such as David Chalmers, who struggle to explain how anything obeying physical laws could be conscious (the Hard Problem). By postulating some new undiscovered physical law of consciousness, the issue becomes a little more manageable.

However, the idea seems unverifiable and there is no physical evidence for such a feature of matter. Moreover, it often serves as a last refuge for the physicalists, who deny anything non-material in the universe. Therefore, it is driven by a worldview (naturalism) not by empirical evidence.

There are many other "isms" related to consciousness. Quantum physics is another rich source of ideas for consciousness. I will show how it fails to provide a satisfactory answer in the chapter about free-will.

Could a computer be conscious?

Could we reproduce consciousness in a computer? Some believe we can. We can create very human-like robots that seem conscious. They answer questions, make decisions, appear to show feelings, and talk to us. Why are they not conscious? After all, what else do you need to show they are conscious beings?

The problem is that computers run on symbols— usually strings of zeros and ones. It is the same with a piece of writing—the symbols convey ideas, but they are not in themselves the ideas. Always, without exception, the ideas come from humans. The philosopher John Searle nailed this by demonstrating that artificial intelligence can never be conscious in his 'Chinese room' thought experiment.[80] It goes like this:

Imagine a computer programmed to simulate the understanding of Chinese. If the computer is given a question in Chinese, it will match the question against its memory, or database, and give the right answers in Chinese. Suppose the computer's responses are indistinguishable from those of a native Chinese speaker. Can we then say the computer understands Chinese in the same way a human does? Searle asks you to imagine that you are locked in a room filled with baskets of Chinese symbols. Imagine that you have no understanding of the Chinese language, but you have a rule book in English for manipulating the Chinese symbols. These rules are for manipulating the symbols according to formal rules; to do with syntax, not the actual meaning. I will quote Searle here:

So the rule might say: 'Take a squiggle-squiggle sign out of basket number one and put it next to a squiggle-squiggle sign from basket number two. Now suppose that some other Chinese symbols are passed into the room, and that you are given further rules for passing back Chinese symbols out of the room. Suppose that unknown to you, the symbols passed into the room are called 'questions' by the people outside the room, and the symbols

---

[80] Searle, J. (1983). Can Computers Think? In Minds, Brains and Science. Cambridge MA. Harvard University Press, pp. 28-41.

you pass back out of the room are called 'answers to the questions.

Searle then imagines a situation where the 'programmers' are so good at designing programs and you become so good at manipulating the symbols that very soon your answers are indistinguishable from those of a native Chinese speaker. Notice that by doing this manipulation of symbols according to rules, you are not learning any Chinese whatsoever.

Essentially, this shows that no computer can understand Chinese, even if it produces answers that seem perfect and as good as a native speaker. There is no actual comprehension by the computer at all.

By the way, quantum computers, once they are developed, will run on symbols (qubits). This is no different from the zeros and ones we currently use in programs, even though at a much faster speed. They could not be conscious.

Searle has demolished any idea that a computer 'understands' in the way you and I do.

As Thomas Nagel has written: *'Eventually, I believe, current attempts to understand the mind by analogy with man-made computers that can perform superbly some of the same external tasks as conscious beings will be recognized as a gigantic waste of time.'* [81]

---

[81] Thomas Nagel (1989). The View from Nowhere. Oxford University Press, p.16.

Neuroscience and the brain

What about MRI scans of the brain? A functional MRI scan shows areas of the brain that are used for different mental states. Surely, this demonstrates that the brain is the very source of such mental states.

It is true that certain areas of the brain are involved in specific types of thinking and a functional MRI proves this. However, this does not show that mental states *are* simply those areas of the brain working alone. This is where the concepts of identity and correlation are really important to grasp. The physical brain state is correlated with certain thoughts, but this does not mean it *is* those thoughts or the primary origin of those thoughts.

In this chapter, we have explored how consciousness is non-physical, so neural networks in the brain could never be identical to consciousness itself. Indeed, no one has yet examined neural tissue and explained how consciousness arises from it. I may see a car driving past in the distance, too far away to see any driver. I could conclude that the car is driving itself based on the limited information. However, I would miss the fact that a driver is the one in charge. It would be foolish of me to conclude that the car is functioning alone. In the same way, the brain is needed for consciousness; it is correlated with consciousness, but this does not mean it **is** consciousness.

Given the nature of consciousness that we have examined, it is more reasonable to conclude that there is an overall person within each of us that is not purely physical. This aligns well with the concept of the soul or person as distinct from the body.

Evolution

As always, evolutionary theorists must come up with some sort of survival value for any aspect of our nature. Consciousness, they say, must have been beneficial for survival on the African savannah. The question is: why is it beneficial? Evolutionary theory requires that every adaptation is for survival and the transfer of genes. Why would consciousness be needed for this? In fact, it is hard to see how consciousness would be helpful in survival. A non-conscious, zombie-like creature could just have easily survived and reproduced, possibly more effectively. A creature lacking consciousness would be arguably better adapted at fulfilling the ruthless survival and reproduction requirements of Evolutionary Theory. Machine-like, they would be rather invincible. There is nothing in Darwinian Theory that requires consciousness and there is no mechanism proposed to account for it.

Here is Thomas Nagel again: '*Without consciousness the mind-body problem would be much less interesting. With consciousness it seems hopeless.*'[82]

---

[82] Thomas, Nagel (1991). Mortal Questions: Canto. Cambridge University Press, p. 166.

What the Bible says

The Bible makes it clear in many places that we, as persons, survive the death of the body.

When Rachel, Jacob's wife was dying in childbirth, we read in Genesis 35:18: *"And as her soul was departing (for she was dying), she called his name Ben-oni; but his father called him Benjamin."* Her soul was departing while her body was laid in the earth. It is still there, but she is not.

The dying thief on the cross put his faith in Jesus who said in Luke 23:43: *"Truly, I say to you, today you will be with me in paradise."* Here, we have the fact that he, as a person, was going to be separated, at least for some time, from his body and would be with Jesus.

In Acts chapter 7, we read that Steven, as he was being stoned to death saw Jesus as the heavens opened. As he died, he cried out: *"Lord Jesus, receive my spirit."* He knew he was going to be with Jesus while his body lay battered and dead.

There is then the fact that we are made in his image. God himself is not physical, but has thoughts, intentions and emotions. He has a mind, however vast and incomprehensible this is to us. We too, in his image, have minds that are non-physical.

We read in John 4:24 the words of Jesus: *"God is Spirit, and those who worship him must worship in spirit and truth."*

In Matthew 10:28, Jesus says: *"And do not fear those who kill the body but cannot kill the soul."* He clearly differentiates the body and the soul and implies that the soul survives the death of the body.

Studying consciousness is not just an academic exercise; it makes us realise the mystery and wonder of what a human being is. I hope that this summary will encourage you in a world where blind and purposeless physicalism seems to reign. Every person is a soul.

CHAPTER 9

FREE WILL

The problem of free will is one of the most fascinating in Philosophy. As humans, we act and feel as if we have free-will. We make informed choices all the time and have the 'freedom' to decide on a variety of actions. Right now, as a trivial example, I can decide freely (so I believe) to continue typing or to go and have a cup of coffee.

Based on this presumed freedom, we assume that we are responsible for our actions. This is where morality is involved; if someone acts in a way that is morally wrong (in our opinion), like killing someone who is innocent, then we feel strongly that some form of punishment is required because they could have decided not to kill. We feel this way even if the background of such an individual has been hard or abusive. Likewise, we feel strongly that we should praise and reward those who do something very good against the odds. We admire and praise them because we know they could have done otherwise. Our praise for good actions and our condemnation of bad actions are wholly dependent on our belief in free-will; hence, it becomes our personal responsibility.

Free will is fascinating in that if we are nothing but material objects then we should not have such freedom. This will become clear as we go on, but it relates to the fact that all physical things are subject to the laws of cause and effect of physics—and there is no freedom in that.

To unravel this idea, I will explain the main thrust of what is called the 'determinist' argument. The determinist argument opines that if the universe, which includes each one of us, is nothing but the interplay of physical forces locked into the laws of physics, then our brains are part of this system. It means that literally every event, including every event in your brain, is governed by the conditions that existed before. Imagine your brain at time "t". The situation in your brain microseconds later, say at time t^1, will be caused by the earlier conditions that existed at time "t" (both in the brain and the conditions acting on the brain from outside). Every bit of the brain's activity, in a closed physical universe, is determined by the prior micro-physical conditions that preceded it. What preceded the brain event (one that perhaps made you choose the blue instead of the grey socks yesterday) may be very complex. Complexity, however, does not remove the basic idea that physical events, including the firing of brain neurons, are under the laws of physics and cannot be free of them in an entirely physical universe. A purely physical universe must obey the laws of physics. This means that the conditions that existed at the Big Bang determined everything that followed. There followed an unbroken chain of causes and effects. If it were possible to have a super-computer that knew every single fact and variable, it would, in this scenario, be potentially able to predict, from the conditions at the Big Bang, what you had at breakfast today and what your dreams were last night. In such a universe, there is no such thing as free will. We may think there is choice but, in fact, we are locked into a sort of clockwork determinism.

Philosophers have struggled with this and some like A. J. Ayer have contended that the only possible reason for our decisions is either determinism or chance[83]. In other words, there is no actual freedom, and the feeling that we are free is entirely unreliable.

This brings us to the subject of quantum physics. After all, could we not apply our knowledge of

---

[83] Ayer, A. J. (1954). Freedom and Necessity: In Philosophical Essays. Macmillan.

indeterminism of quantum events to our understanding of free will? Quantum events, at the atomic level, are not predictable even though they follow certain laws of probability. Does this not allow for freedom in brain activity? At the micro-physical or quantum level, we can imagine a less deterministic process. This might seem to rescue us from the clockwork cause and effect of determinism.

However, an unpredictable quantum world, even if under certain laws of probability, does not allow for any real freedom. Freedom of will requires freedom—not some physical system, however complex, that makes the state of the brain unpredictable.

Determinists are faithful to the idea that everything in the universe is under physical laws. To them, there is no non-physical entity; there cannot be a free-willing non-physical mind. Some, such as Susan Blackmore, try to live as if there is no free will and consciously attempt to 'allow' the mind to go its own way.[84]

There are also some philosophers, known as compatibilists, who genuinely believe in determinism but also think that free-will is possible, despite this. I will not go into their arguments because I believe they are unreasonable and unfounded.

There is a great deal at stake here. To go down the materialist road requires us to ditch our freedom, freedom of choice for which there is much evidence in

---

[84] See Blackmore, Susan. (2005). Conversations on Consciousness. Oxford University Press, p. 207.

our daily lives. It requires us to abandon any moral judgement on behaviour. Hitler could not have done anything else but murder Jews. Are we willing to agree to this? Most materialists do not wish to face this or are ignorant of the consequences.

In a deterministic world, there is no morality in human actions. We may feel that something is bad but not punishable. The murderer perhaps should be locked up to keep us safe but not punished or in any way blamed[85]. Nor is there any place surely for praise or admiration for 'good' actions. The soldier who wins the V.C. does not deserve it any more than the coward who runs from the fight. We are machines at the mercy of physical circumstances that is all.

I believe that such a materialist position is one of obstinacy in the face of facts about humans as real persons with freedom to choose. It is a position which depends on the '*a priori*' denial of anything other than the physical—not on evidence. Our scientific instruments are made to look at the physical world and it is hardly surprising therefore that the non-physical is undetectable by them. Meanwhile, a careful examination of how our minds really function gives us a wealth of evidence for something other than the mere firing of neurons.

And so, the evidence does point to real freedom, real responsibility and real meaning in our thoughts and

---

[85] This was the opinion of J. C. Smart in his 'Free Will, Praise and Blame' from Mind (1961), 70: 291-306.

decisions. I believe the consistency of how people behave demonstrates this. If determinism is true, then there is no such thing as a good or bad way of thinking. Thinking would follow physics and not morality. Even the belief that determinism is true is self-contradictory; you have no control over such a belief in this scenario.

This is where the study of free-will actually leads us to a very reasonable conclusion: that our minds are non-physical. This is the only way in which there can be genuine freedom of thought. The alternative is that we are locked into a physical deterministic hopelessness (or in the case of quantum events, unpredictability)—where we have no real choices, and we have no real responsibility.

The mind or soul is not physical and the study of free-will adds more evidence for this conclusion.

Of course, this leads us to ask where such a non-physical soul/mind comes from. It leads us inevitably to a non-physical mind, that of our Creator.

CHAPTER 10

THE MORAL ARGUMENT FOR GOD

What are moral values, and where do they come from? Most of us think that cheating in exams, stealing and murdering are wrong. We also believe that helping our neighbours is good. In fact, we base our lives and judgements of others, on these beliefs. Our prisons are full of people who we think have broken these values.

You may say that such values are simply personal opinions, with no particular reference outside of ourselves. However, this seems inconsistent with the fact that usually such values are shared by others. It would be hard to find anyone who thinks torturing children is acceptable. You may then say that such beliefs are culturally based. We could point out that different cultures have differing values. Slavery, for instance, has been considered perfectly acceptable by many cultures. I will examine this argument later in the chapter.

Others will argue that moral values are innate and having such values enables us to survive and reproduce. If there were no proper values, then life would be chaotic and our fitness to pass on our genes would be compromised.

What I hope will become clear in this chapter is that, while there is a grain of truth in all these answers, none is adequate to explain morality. They are what is termed '*subjectivist*' views. In other words, they deny that moral values are independent of ourselves, our communities or our genes. There is no place in any of these views for some independent objective reality to moral values. My aim in this chapter is to show that moral values are *objective* and 'out there'—not just personal opinion, not just programmed into our genes, not just culturally imbibed.

Why is this important? Because if moral rules are objective, given, independent of us—then we have to ask, how did they come to be and who made them?

The evolutionary approach

Charles Darwin, in his book 'The Descent of Man', tried to account for moral tendencies by assuming that natural selection has honed these over many generations to maximise the survival of the species.

He wrote: *"In however complex a manner this feeling may have originated, as it is one of high importance to all those animals which aid and defend one another. It will have been increased through Natural Selection; for those communities, which included the greatest number of the most sympathetic members, would flourish best and rear the greatest number of offspring."*[86]

Despite this, he struggled to accommodate this view with the fact that he believed slavery to be wrong. You see, slavery, in evolutionary terms, is very beneficial to those who practice it. One would think that we should have been hard-wired by evolution to promote slavery, but Darwin knew that slavery is simply, in itself, intrinsically wrong.

He also, very honestly, struggled to explain behaviours such as sacrificing one's life for others in a battle. How could this lead to survival of one's genes? Modern evolutionists have tried to answer this problem; let us examine what they say.

For example, Richard Dawkins, in his book 'The God Delusion'[87], tries to tackle the question of morals

---

[86] Darwin, C. (1871). The Descent of Man and Selection in Relation to Sex. Part 1. London: William Pickering.

[87] Dawkins, R. (2006). The God Delusion. London: Bantam Press.

in his chapter 'Why are we good'? He gives two main reasons for why he and many others believe that morality is programmed into our genes by evolution.

The first reason given is that helping others, particularly those related to us, ensures the survival of the shared genes we have within our immediate kin group. In other words, if we protect our immediate family or relations, who share our genes, we will encourage the copying of those genes into future generations. This could even involve sacrificing one's own life to save our relations, for by doing so the genes shared with our family are more likely to be passed on.

Notice here how he reduces us to machines, merely obeying those molecules called genes. It is the ultimate subjectivist view. There is nothing absolute or 'real' about such morals, just selfish genes programming us to pass on as many of those genes as possible. In this Neo-Darwinist view, held almost religiously by some, our consciences are simply hard-wired by DNA. There is no reason for thinking something is good or bad other than genetic survival. We should reflect on this and realise how bleak it is.

His second reason for why evolution has programmed us for morality is known as *Reciprocal Altruism*. The idea is that if you help others, you may get help in return. Scratch my back and I might scratch yours. All this is coded in our genes in order to make survival and reproduction more likely. Once more, we see only blind molecules somehow, as if conscious, striving for supremacy and survival. And so, if I help another person, what seems genuinely good and admirable, is merely slavery to bits of DNA. It is once again, pure subjectivism with nothing genuinely real about our good actions. There is no virtue in this scenario.

He then adds some further evolutionary reasons for good behaviour: good actions ensure our reputation is increased and improve our status or dominance in society. Remember that all these evolutionary reasons for good behaviour are entirely selfish and are ruthlessly about genetic survival—and nothing else.

Does this Darwinist answer to the origin of morals stand up to scrutiny? Sometimes, we need to test such views with extreme examples. For example, was the holocaust wrong? To Dawkins, our answer (that it was wrong) is merely a genetic programming. Our revulsion concerning the holocaust may feel genuine, but it is not based on any actual evil and is merely somehow our DNA making us feel that way. Do you buy that?

The holocaust, of course, was simply evil, full-stop. Genes have nothing to do with this assessment. It was objectively wrong.

Zoologist Matt Ridley, in his book 'The Origins of Virtue'[88], agrees with Dawkins. He writes: *"If a mother is selfless towards her offspring only because her genes are being selfish, she is still, as an individual, behaving selflessly."*

In other words, he maintains that a mother's self-sacrificial love for her child is programmed by genes,

---

[88] Ridley, M. (1997). The Origins of Virtue. Penguin.

but somehow this is fine, and she is *actually* being selfless. However, how can we accept this as 'fine'? The mother is merely acting and feeling love for her child as if she were a computer running off software. It is mechanistic, heartless, and unreal. It is a con trick played by selfish genes. Are you not disturbed by this reduction of morals to genetic code?

Philosopher Anthony O'Hear, is helpful here. In his book 'Beyond Evolution'[89], he writes about the death of Socrates, who willingly died rather than give up his principles:

If it is said that from the evolutionary point of view, Socrates was a failure, and that a nation of Socrateses would not survive…this still does not explain why Socrates is so widely admired a figure, and why many people even today, and in quite different social and religious circumstances, feel that Socrates was right to have done what he had done.

What O'Hear is pointing out here is that evolutionary genetic programming can never explain something like the death of Socrates. It was a death, which in evolutionary terms was disastrous for the survival of his genes. Yet, his death is held up by most as exemplary. Ultimately, the Darwinist explanation fails to provide reasons for such widely admired self-sacrifice.

The Christian story of Jesus, willingly dying on a cross for us, leaving no physical descendants, is the

---

[89] O'Hear, A. (1997). Beyond Evolution. Human Nature and the Limits of Evolutionary Explanation. Oxford: Oxford University Press.

greatest narrative in history. This act of self-sacrifice, which has so changed the world, is more revered than any other. Evolutionary selfishness cannot explain this. If we are merely duped by our genes, then we would roundly condemn his death and strive never to emulate such selflessness, but the best part of us does strive to emulate Him.

Ultimately, the Darwinist explanation fails to provide reasons for such self-sacrifice. It cannot explain altruism, which is selfless, and has no bearing on the survival of one's genes. It denies anything real about good and bad – just genetic hardwiring making us think some things are good and others bad or evil.

Nietzsche understood this. Although he did not accept all of Darwin's theory, he found within it support for his atheism and his denial that moral values exist (apart from 'the will to power'). As H. James Birx wrote about Nietzsche:

In fact, this philosopher held that Darwinian evolution led to a collapse of all traditional values because both objective meaning and spiritual purpose had vanished from reality (and consequently, there can be no fixed or certain morality).[90]

Other arguments for subjectivism

One argument used to defend subjectivism is that different groups hold different beliefs. Killing cows is

---

[90] Birx, H. J. (2000). Nietzche and Evolution Philosophy Now. Issue 29.

wrong in some cultures, whereas in others it is right. Abortion is seen as a good thing by some people while others see it as wrong. So, the argument goes that if there is such variation in moral beliefs, there cannot be any real objective right or wrong.

The problem with this argument is this: disagreement about certain things does not mean there is no actual truth. For example, as Peter S. Williams writes[91], brilliant physicists disagree about some of the fundamental laws of nature. This does not mean there is no *actual truth* about those laws.

A second argument used to defend subjectivism is that claiming objective truth about moral values condemns people with opposing views. It somehow lacks the acceptance of the other person. In other words, objectivism maintains that there is some real truth that we can argue about, and this diminishes the person who has alternative beliefs. This is a modern (or post-modern) sentiment that we should simply accept the beliefs of others.

Firstly, the claim that there are objective moral values does not in itself condemn anyone who disagrees. Secondly, the objectivist does not say that his or her *particular* views are always right or forced on others—just that moral values do have objective truth.

In fact, subjectivism stifles proper debate. If there is no real truth about moral values, then we cannot argue

---

[91] Williams, Peter S. (2013). A Faithful Guide to Philosophy. Paternoster.

against or defend such values. The debates about slavery, which Wilberforce had in parliament, would be seen as ridiculous if we follow the subjectivist line. It was by debate and the evidence given that won the day for the abolition of slavery.

C.S. Lewis wrote: *"The Law of right and wrong must be something above and beyond the actual facts of human behaviour. In this case, besides the actual facts, you have something else – a real law which we did not invent and which we know we ought to obey."*[92]

Utilitarianism

One of the principal and most popular forms of ethics is that of utilitarianism. Essentially, it is an ethic that judges any action by the consequences of that action, in the form of human happiness or well-being in the future. Utilitarianism is less interested in the means and more in the ends. Of course, it is a good thing to attempt to predict the outcome of our actions, but to ignore the *means* by which this is achieved is very questionable. An extreme example of utilitarian ethic was the way Nazi doctors experimented on prisoners in concentration camps. In a utilitarian world, they could, and did, justify such torture by predicting good outcomes, and the overall benefit for medical practice in the future.

Utilitarianism is arguably very linked to moral subjectivism. If we do not have any objective yardstick

[92] Lewis, C.S. (2001). Mere Christianity. London: HarperCollins.

as to what is right and wrong, then we are more likely to justify bad actions if they are supposed to lead to good outcomes.

The Euthyphro dilemma

This "dilemma" is used by atheists to undermine the goodness of God (and therefore of God as a good giver of moral laws). It is an exceptionally poor argument.

It is derived from a discussion of Plato about what goodness is, by asking whether a thing is good because God says it is good, or does God say it is good because it is good. This is put forward as a dilemma. The argument goes as follows:

1. If a thing is good because God says it is good, then it seems that God could say anything is good, even evil things.

2. If God is simply reporting a thing's goodness, then he is no longer the standard for goodness.

This is argued by atheists as if these are the only options. What is omitted is the very obvious alternative that God is the author of goodness, the very source of goodness. As the Bible says, 'God is love'.[93] Goodness does not depend on his fickle opinion, and He is not simply reporting what is good, independent of Himself.

---

[93] 1 John 4:16

Beauty

There is a close link between what is beautiful and what is good. In the first chapter of Genesis, there is a repeated refrain after the acts of creation: *"And God saw that it was good."* The word used for good here is closely linked to that of beauty.

If the world and the universe is beautiful (and it clearly is), independent of our opinions about it, as I will argue in the chapter on beauty—then this also points to the reality of objective goodness.

What does this say about God?

If there is no God, then, the universe is, as the atheist believes, a collection of matter and energy. There would be no purpose or ultimate meaning in this. There would be no absolute values or objective morality. In such a universe, there would be nothing beyond mere physics that gives us any rules about what is good or bad. Goodness and badness then become matters of opinion or evolutionary programming.

Yet, as we have seen, there are very good reasons for believing in objective goodness and badness. The holocaust was evil. Torturing children is evil. The list goes on. Loving our neighbour is good, not simply because it increases our likelihood of passing our genes on but because we intuitively know this is true. Intuition is an often maligned source of truth. We should not deride it, as Iain McGilchrist has very effectively shown.[94]

Since objective moral values exist, we must conclude there is a good moral law-giver. The God of the Bible fulfils this perfectly. He is not simply good but supremely so. So good that he came to earth and died on a cross for us.

This subject is of vital importance in a time when there is a prevalent utilitarian and subjectivist mindset in Western society. We seem to have lost the transcendent nature of morality and are left to making our own rules. There is no real yardstick. Where is the moral compass? That which is sacred is trampled on.

Understanding the reality of moral values, which can only come from a perfect and good source, is a very powerful way to return the doubting sceptic to God, who is the only reasonable source of what is good and excellent.

What about evil and suffering?

This is not the place to write extensively about such an important subject. It is not a trivial question: how can a good God allow evil and suffering?

Regarding human evil, there is the argument that God allows us free-will because he has made us responsible beings, not robots. Therefore, we are given

---

[94] McGilchrist, I. (2023). The Matter with Things. Our Brains, Our Delusions, and the Unmaking of the World. Perspectiva.

the freedom to do good or bad. Evil, in the Bible, is never God's will and will be judged.

Regarding natural causes of suffering, the Bible teaches that we are in a fallen universe that will one day be restored. We may not understand this (and we don't), but natural causes of suffering—disease and disaster, are alien to what the original creation was meant to be.

Probably the most impressive reason to believe that God is altogether good, abhors evil, and fully enters into our suffering—is the life and death of Jesus. If God himself came to earth and died brutally on a cross out of love for us, then we can believe that He himself is willing to suffer and live out his love for us completely and sacrificially.

Moreover, when we struggle and sigh as we see the obvious evils and great suffering in our world, we at the same time uphold the fact that these things go against the objective goodness that we aspire to and wish for all people. We struggle with it because we feel deep down that these evils should not be. This has nothing to do with differing opinions, or genetic programming. We are genuinely distraught when we see evil done to and suffered by others because there is such a thing as objective goodness.

The teaching of Jesus on morality

It is in the Sermon on the Mount[95] in Matthew's gospel that we get a close look at what I mean by the goodness

---

[95] Matthew chapters 5-7

of God. Here, Jesus lays out for us what perfection really is in the life of a human being; a perfection which none of us actually achieves in this life, but which he achieved.

At the very start, he tells us who is blessed—not the rich nor the comfortable nor the self-satisfied. It is the *poor in spirit, those who mourn, the meek, those who hunger and thirst after righteousness, the merciful, the pure in heart, the peacemakers,* and *those who are persecuted for righteousness' sake.* It is revolutionary teaching.

We are to be salt of the earth and light in the world.

If we are angry with our brother, it is likened to killing him in God's sight.

It is not just the physical acts of adultery that matter but lust, which is the adultery of the heart.

He says: "*Do not resist the one who is evil. But if anyone slaps you on the right cheek, turn to him the other also.*"

If we are compelled by someone to go one mile, we should go two miles with them.

We must give to the one who begs from us. (This surely is a principal, an ideal—and requires deeper 'giving' than simply handing every beggar what they ask for. We should ask: what is the greatest need of the beggar?)

We are to love our enemies and pray for those who persecute us.

We are to avoid all show or hypocrisy.

We must not judge others: he says "*Why do you see the speck that is in your brother's eye but do not notice the log that is in your own eye.*"

Whatever you wish others to do to you, we must do also to them.

The crowd on the side of the mountain knew that they were in the presence of someone with immense authority and we read:

"And when Jesus finished these sayings, the crowds were astonished at his teaching, for he was teaching them as one who had authority, and not as their scribes."[96]

We see in the life of Jesus the actual playing out, uniquely, of this moral code. And when he was being nailed to a cross, he prayed: *"Father, forgive them, for they know not what they do."*[97] He loved and prayed for his enemies.

---

[96] Matthew 7:28-29
[97] Luke 23:34

CHAPTER 11

BEAUTY

When we look at something beautiful, such as a rainbow, a magnificent landscape, a cheetah running or an eagle soaring—what is actually happening? Is this merely a personal experience that our brain interprets as lovely? Or, is there beauty there whether anyone is looking or not? In other words, do beautiful things have intrinsic beauty, quite independently from any observer?

This is important because if beauty exists in a thing itself, regardless of any onlooker, we have to ask where it comes from. What gives it beauty? The atheist generally denies any objectivity in beauty. This is because to acknowledge that things are *really* beautiful, in themselves, inevitably leads to the author of beauty, God.

I live in a particularly beautiful part of the world and I literally drink in the beauty that surrounds me. Most people understand this. The beauty certainly seems real, not simply made up by my brain. It is the same way when we look at great arts. Very often, it exudes beauty. We stand within the Sistine chapel, or before a Turner painting and we acknowledge the beauty. The question is, are we duped by our senses to just feel they are beautiful?

Mathematicians speak of the beauty of equations. When an equation opens up the realities of the universe, it is spoken of in awe as beautiful. Indeed, many physicists would not accept that such an equation is valid unless it is beautiful.

In my book about biology, The Naked Emperor[98], I wrote the following:

"I believe that flowers are really beautiful and therefore their beauty has an objective reality. If not, then the rose has no more beauty than a piece of coal or a rusty nail."

One philosopher wrote:

---

[98] Latham, A. (2005). The Naked Emperor: Darwinism Exposed. Janus.

"Just as my experience of roundness when I look at an orange is not in itself round, my experience of aesthetic excellence has an objective reference beyond the experience itself."[99]

Yet, modern thinkers have relegated beauty to mere feelings in ourselves. This is the view of most atheists. Richard Dawkins out rules a creator; to him, science has emancipated us. He said the following in a debate with John Lennox[100]:

I think that when you consider the beauty of the world and you wonder how it came to be what it is, you are naturally overwhelmed with a feeling of awe, a feeling of admiration and you almost feel a desire to worship something. I feel this, I recognise that other scientists feel (such as Carl Sagan) feel this. Einstein felt it. We, all of us, share a kind of religious reverence for the beauties of the universe, for the complexity of life, and for the sheer magnitude of geological time. And it's tempting to translate that feeling of awe and worship into a desire to worship some particular thing, a person, or an agent. You want to attribute it to a maker, a creator. What science has now achieved is an emancipation from that impulse to attribute these things to a creator.

Dawkins never actually explains how science has done this.

---

[99] Douglas, G. (2000). Truth Decay. Downers Grove, IL: IVP. P. 257.

[100] Dawkins, R. (2007). In 'God Delusion' debate with John Lennox.

ANTONY LATHAM

Here are some of the arguments put forward by
atheists:

1. Evolution: The message is that our appreciation of
beauty has survival value. An experience of beauty
enhances reproduction and the transmission of our
genes. Somehow, the good feelings of beauty enhance
relationships, well-being and harmony—leading more
likely to reproduction and genetic success.

We see the way this is going—it is important for
some to give evolution the credit for just about
everything about us. However, it is a great deal to ask us
to believe that a sunset, the song of birds, and the sound
of wind on the sea are necessary, at all, in the brute
business of passing on our genes.

We also have to ask why evolution has chosen some
things to be beautiful and not others—if there is no real
difference, intrinsically.

Have you noticed how beautiful the cosmos is, as
seen by telescopes? The more we see of the galaxies and
the exploding supernovas, the more amazed we are. Yet,
no evolutionary process was able to prepare us for this.
Our ancestors did not have telescopes. The fact that the
cosmos appears beautiful indicates that it **is** actually
beautiful.

2. The philosopher may also say that colour and
appearance are merely the our brains interpret
certain patterns and wavelengths of light. The objects
themselves do not give out this light, they only reflect

the light. And so, the argument is that only the interpretation of the light by the brain is beautiful.

But, how else can we experience what is beautiful except through our senses? The experience of beauty, what we often feel with awe, must have its origin in the object. Other objects are not beautiful – so there is a difference in the objects we view, that can only be in them objectively. Indeed, if we are created, then we would expect to be given the equipment in our minds to know what is actually out there in the world.

3. There are cultural differences in the appreciation of beauty. For example, the music of China does not immediately sound beautiful to me. The argument then is that the experience of beauty is all relative and not really objective.

Yet, we fiercely defend our belief that something is beautiful. I may not appreciate Chinese music, but a Chinese person will try hard to show me why it is beautiful and with persistence and exposure to it, I will indeed learn to appreciate it—because it is objectively beautiful. Therefore, differences in opinion about beauty do not invalidate the reality of it. Mostly we agree. No one says rainbows are ugly.

The argument for God from beauty

If we accept that beauty is indeed out there, objectively, then we must ask why.

There must be an objective standard of beauty that is independent of our minds. This standard cannot be physical because a standard of beauty is a value, and values, like moral values, are not physical things. There is something personal about beauty. What or who is this personal origin of beauty?

Descartes wrote: "*Now, it is manifest by natural light that there must be as much reality in the efficient and total cause as in its effect; for whence can the effect draw its reality if not from the cause?*"[101]

Descartes was referring to his *concept* of God being an effect of the real cause, God himself. But the same reasoning can be used to attribute the objective reality of immense beauty to a cause—a beautiful creator.

There must be a first cause of beauty. Such a cause needs to be personal and, it can be argued, must be maximally beautiful. God fulfils this description exactly. All arts have personal creators. The universe is no different in this respect.

The great Scottish mountaineer and writer, W. H. Murray wrote about his experience one day on the top of the Cuillin Ridge, Isle of Skye:

The grey sky was changing to cornflower blue and black rock to ashen. To obtain a still finer vantage point, we moved east to Sgurr a'Mhadaidh. No sooner did we reach the top than the sun rose. Down in the basin of Coruisk, the cloud-surface at once flashed into flame, as though a stupendous crucible were filled with burning silver. The twenty turrets of the Cuillin, like

---

[101] Descartes, R. (1641). Meditations on First Philosophy. 1985 Edition: Cambridge University Press.

islands lapped by fire-foam, flushed faintly pink. The shade crimsoned. Within a space of minutes, the rocks had run the gamut of autumn leafage, 'yellow, and black, and pale, and hectic red.'

*Beyond such bare words, one may say little. The mind fails one miserably and painfully before great beauty. It cannot understand. Yet, it would contain more. Mercifully, it is by this very process of not understanding that one is allowed to understand much: for each one of us has within him 'the divine reason that sits at the helm of the soul', of which the head knows nothing. Find beauty; be still; and that faculty grows more surely than a grain sown in season.*102

As we have already seen in the first chapter of Genesis, in the account of creation, we read repeatedly after a phase of the creative work: *"And God saw that it was good."* This word 'good' can also have the meaning of beautiful in Hebrew. What God made was and is beautiful. Nature has his personal, beautiful stamp upon it.

The post-modern rejection of objective beauty and value is a logical consequence of rejection of God. This accounts for the relativism that pervades much thought: whatever you believe in is just as good as what anyone else does. Art itself has become, often, divorced from any idea of objective beauty—frequently despairing, ugly and futile.

---

102 Murray W.H. (1951). Mountaineering in Scotland. 2022 edition. Vertebrate Publishing, p. 4.

It is worth remembering that beautiful psalm:

"One thing I have asked of the Lord that I will seek after: that I may dwell in the house of the Lord all the days of my life, to gaze upon the beauty of the Lord and to enquire in his temple."[103]

Only a belief in God can account for beauty; beauty that is personal and emanates from perfect beauty.

---

[103] Psalm 27:4

CHAPTER 12

AN OPEN UNIVERSE

What seems to be a stumbling block to many atheists is the idea of miracles. Surely, since we have left the dark ages (the argument goes), we have to ditch anything that is not natural. Science seems to have uncovered so many secrets that, to posit some force or being outside of what is empirical and measurable, appears simply wrong. After all, even Newton was confused about this—he thought God was needed to correct the orbits of some of the planets now and then to keep them in place. We now know that is not needed—they simply obey physical laws.

This worldview is common and is often termed 'methodological naturalism'. I held it for a while when I was young. It is tempting and seems to make some sense. Why put God into the gaps in our knowledge? Those gaps in our knowledge are growing smaller all the time—*or so it seems*. The methodological naturalist, sometimes called the materialist or physicalist, believes that there is *only* matter and energy, and nothing else.

Such a view only stands scrutiny if the universe can be proved to be *uncreated* and is *causally closed*. 'Causal closure' means that the universe is somehow sealed from any outside influence, in particular any influence by the Creator. Those who believe in this hold that only natural laws can be the cause of events. Nothing outside intervenes.

The premise for this belief in Methodological Naturalism is wrong on two main counts:

Firstly, countering the idea that we are uncreated, science has actually uncovered remarkable evidence for design and purpose in the universe. We have seen how there is clear evidence that there was a beginning, demanding a cause outside the universe. The fact that there is 'something rather than nothing' requires an unmoved first mover. The universe is also stunningly fine-tuned for life. Evolutionary theory does not answer how life began, how macro-evolution occurs, how life is replete with irreducibly complexity, and how our DNA is packed with meaningful, intentional and specified information. The human mind has all the hallmarks of being immaterial and we have seen that the moral law that we all have is objective, requiring a law giver. Moreover, the evidence of a creator from the sheer beauty in the universe is overwhelming.

The hubris surrounding the idea of scientists one day fully describing and understanding it all is rudely punctured by the study of the quantum world. This shows us things that are simply inexplicable in human terms, and which lead, if we are honest to humble awe. Rather than assuming we are getting to the nuts and bolts of things, the subatomic world of particle physics is a zoo of strangeness.

Now I know there are those who strive to one day fully understand the quantum world, but it is worth at least looking at some of the facts. Firstly, there is the superposition of particles, which can be in more than one position at the same time until we measure them. Secondly, there is the nature of light as both waves *and* particles. Lastly, there is the entanglement of particles, whose properties, such as polarisation or spin, are so correlated that it appears, as Einstein famously described it as 'spooky action at a distance'.

There is also the fact that if we know the position of a particle at a particular moment, we can never determine its position at later time (unlike straightforward Newtonian physics). We can only give probabilities of where that particle may end up—never certainty. We do not understand the quantum world even if we can (and do) use the equations successfully all the time.

Neils Bohr, who was responsible for developing the quantum theory more than anyone else, was convinced that the subatomic world was always going to be incomprehensible to us said:

"There is no quantum world. There is only an abstract quantum physical description."[104]

Nobel laureate physicist Richard Feynman famously said:

"If you think you understand quantum mechanics, you don't understand quantum mechanics."

The originator of quantum theory, Max Plank, wrote:

"Science cannot solve the ultimate mystery of nature. And that is because, in the last analysis, we ourselves are a part of that mystery that we are trying to solve."[105]

Therefore, scientists need to accept that there are things which will always be mysterious. Humility before the facts we do know and realising what we cannot know leads us away from methodological naturalism and its assumptions, towards a cause beyond mere matter and energy. As Hamlet says, when Horatio describes seeing a ghost:

---

[104] Petersen, A. (1963). The Philosophy of Niels Bohr. Bulletin of the Atomic Scientists. Vol xix (7), p.12.

[105] Plank, M. (1932). Where is Science Going? 1981 Ed. Ox Bow Press.

"There are more things in heaven and earth, Horatio, than are dreamt of in your philosophy."[106]

Secondly, relating to the title of this chapter, methodological naturalism depends on a great assumption—that our universe is causally closed[107]. A closed physical system is one that *only* has actions and causes within itself and no outside force or power can affect it. Indeed, methodological naturalism would be true if such a closed system existed—there would be nothing but its own physical laws and conditions. All would be just material. The problem with this view is that there is no proof of it and it is a belief—not verified by science.

The Christian view, and that of many in other religions, maintains that the universe is not causally closed and that God, who is not physical, does act upon and within it. This is theism. We have seen in the previous chapters how physicalism fails on many counts, empirically and rationally. We have no idea why the laws of physics are exactly as they are, but if created then they are not inviolable to the creator. Indeed, we have every reason to expect the hand of a creator, who formed the universe out of nothing, acting freely within the cosmos to perform what we call miracles.

---

[106] Shakespeare by W. Hamlet
[107] See good coverage of this in: Shakespeare. W. Hamlet (2011). Where the Conflict Really Lies: Science, Religion, & Naturalism? Oxford University Press.

The physicist may object that one cannot break certain laws such as the law of conservation of energy and this indeed would be true in a completely closed system. But if the system is *not* causally closed, then this objection is groundless. The belief in a causally closed universe is a belief, not science.

Methodological Naturalism, which leads to 'scientism' (only science can describe the world), is a philosophy that everything must be measurable and according to fixed, inviolate laws of nature in an entirely physical, causally closed universe. Ultimately, it uses a circular argument based on a belief:

1. There is nothing but matter and energy and therefore all is physical.

2. Therefore, we must base our understanding only on physical measurements according to the laws of nature.

3. Therefore, anything outside such a universe is impossible.

You can see how a pure belief (premise 1) leads to a conclusion (2), which leads to an assertion (3). The premise of 1 is however a belief, not a fact and the argument is circular.

There are theologians who also baulk at the idea of God intervening in nature. They want a God who is uniform. It seems that they cannot accept the idea of God overturning his own laws. I have had discussions with Christian scientists who cannot abide the idea of God 'tinkering' with his creation.

This would be reasonable if God's interventions were arbitrary. But theism is the belief, not just that God upholds and sustains everything constantly (which of course is a form of intervention), but that he intervenes purposely when he has a good reason. This is what miracles are.

Science and miracles are perfectly compatible.

CHAPTER 13

THE EVIDENCE FOR THE RESURRECTION OF JESUS

If naturalism fails to account for what we know about the universe, then we should use our rational minds to examine miracles. The most debated miracle in history is surely the resurrection of Jesus. If the physical resurrection of Jesus happened, then naturalism is false.

Soon after I had become a Christian, a good friend of mine asked me if he needed to believe in the resurrection to be a Christian. I probably mumbled an inadequate reply to this but it is a really good question.

Christianity stands or falls on this matter. If Jesus did not rise from the dead, then the gospel of a living Lord who is with his people now, as the New Testament proclaims, is completely torpedoed, as is our own hope of a life after death with him.

Paul the apostle put it this way in his first letter to the Corinthian church: *"If in Christ we have hope in this life only, we are of all people most to be pitied."*[108]

We need to have a serious look at the evidence.

He was crucified

We can say for certain that he was crucified. We have eyewitness accounts of this in the gospels, which are very accurate as to the nature of crucifixion and all agree with one another. They were written only a few years after the event. These disciples were willing to die for proclaiming this.

Moreover, the celebration of Holy Communion or the Lord's Supper, began at the beginning of the church, the taking of bread and the wine symbolising the body and the blood of Jesus, sacrificed for us on the cross.

There is also the fact that if the disciples wanted to make up stories about their Lord, they would not have chosen to have him crucified—the most degrading and shameful form of execution possible. It is the crucifixion that still causes offence to many people who

---

[108] 1 Corinthians 15:19

cannot understand why God the Son would allow himself to die in this hideous way.

No serious historian doubts that Jesus was crucified. For a good and disturbing description of how the Romans went about this, I recommend reading 'Dominion'[109] by the historian Tom Holland.

He died on the cross

There are then those who doubt that Jesus actually died on the cross. They assert that, somehow, he recovered after being taken down and that the accounts of him being seen alive later, are simply due to this.

This idea that he did not die on the cross completely ignores the fact that the Romans were experts at this vile form of execution. They knew what they were doing. Thousands were crucified around the time of Jesus. Failure to succeed in crucifying someone would lead to severe punishment for the soldiers involved. The idea that he somehow recovered soon after (3 days after) is simply preposterous.

One of the most convincing incidents that we read about the crucifixion occurs in John's gospel. John was present at the crucifixion, along with Mary the mother of Jesus. John writes about what happened when the soldiers wanted to be absolutely sure that he was dead:

---

[109] Holland, T. (2019). Dominian: The Making of the Western Mind. Abacus books.

"But one of the soldiers pierced his side with a spear, and at once, there came out blood and water. He who saw it has borne witness that his testimony is true."[110]

As a doctor, I know that in this situation, following flogging and crucifixion, fluid can build up around the lungs as a pleural effusion. The spear would have released this clear fluid and then entered the heart, from where blood came out. John was a fisherman who would not have known about these underlying facts. His account therefore must be true.

He was put in a tomb

In all four gospels, we have an account of Joseph of Arimathea taking the body of Jesus and putting it into a tomb that he owned nearby. Joseph was a member of the Sanhedrin, the ruling body of the Jews. It was the members of the Sanhedrin who demanded the crucifixion of Jesus. But Joseph, as we read in the accounts, was a secret believer and was willing to take a huge risk in identifying himself with Jesus. It all holds together only if it was an accurate account. Moreover, anyone could check the truth of this; they would not have got away with a made-up story about this very prominent man.

The descriptions of the stone that was rolled over the tomb entrance accord very well with what we know

---

[110] John 19:34-35

about such tombs. These were enormous and heavy, usually disc shaped stones.

The tomb was empty

What is really remarkable is that the accounts in the gospels of the empty tomb and the appearance of Jesus, involve the witness of women. Women in that society were not considered proper witnesses. To base the resurrection story on women's testimony would have been unthinkable to anyone making it all up. It is, therefore, completely believable. The first ones who found the empty tomb, as the gospels recount, were women followers of Jesus. Only the truth would account for this.

One theory is that perhaps the Romans stole the body, and this accounts for the empty tomb. But this does not work—they would have immediately produced the body once the stories of resurrection circulated. No body was produced.

Another idea is that the disciples stole the body to make it seem that he had risen from the tomb. But this means they would have lived a complete lie. These disciples, without exception, were quite willing to proclaim the resurrection of Jesus until the end of their lives. And their lives were nearly all ended violently, dying by execution for those beliefs. It makes no sense to say they made it all up. Human nature does not work that way.

He was seen by many

In the gospels, we have accounts of meetings which Jesus had with his disciples on a number of occasions, after he was crucified. This occurred over several weeks. Remember too that the first ones to see him were women[111]. Once again, it is worth stating that no disciple would make up a story involving women as the first to see him. Their witness counted for nothing in that society.

Paul, in his first letter to the Corinthians, written between AD 55 and 57, states that Jesus appeared after his death to many, including to more than 500 people at one time, and to all the disciples. He says he also appeared to James, the brother of Jesus and lastly to himself. He makes it clear that most of those Jesus appeared to, were still alive when he wrote his letter. Any of these people could have checked and refuted his facts.

In the book of Acts, in the first chapter, we read that Jesus appeared alive to the disciples for forty days, following his crucifixion.

Peter, in his speech to Cornelius, states that he and the other disciples *"…ate and drank with him after he had risen from the dead."*[112]

---

[111] Matthew 28:9, John 20:14
[112] Acts 10:41

They died for their beliefs

I have already mentioned this, but it is worth emphasising that a majority of the disciples were executed as martyrs because they would not stop proclaiming the truth of the risen Jesus. People will die for religious beliefs if they sincerely believe they are true, but people will **not** die for their religious beliefs if they know the beliefs are false.

The willingness of the disciples to die for what they proclaimed and the amazing excitement and joy they had in telling others, shows that their testimony could not have been based on some deliberate hoax that they had cooked up.

The conversion of sceptics

The best-known sceptic was the disciple, Thomas. We read in John's gospel that he simply could not bring himself to believe that the others had seen Jesus alive. It is an account that rings true. Thomas stands for so many who struggle to believe. Yet, when he saw Jesus a week later (John 20), he did not have to put his hands on the nail or spear marks; once he saw him, he simply worshipped and said, *"My Lord and my God."[113]*

We also know that James, the brother of Jesus came to believe and, according to Paul in his first letter to the Corinthians, met with the risen Jesus. James had been a doubter about Jesus, before the crucifixion, along with

---

[113] John 20:28

his other brothers. In John's gospel, we read *"For even his own brothers did not believe in him."*[114] Yet, after he had seen Jesus risen, James became a leader of the church in Jerusalem.

Perhaps the most dramatic conversion of someone who saw Jesus after he was risen was the apostle, Paul. He did everything he could to stamp out Christianity until he saw Jesus and was completely changed as a result—following Jesus until his own execution in Rome.

Personal experience

Countless people, and I include myself, have experienced the risen Jesus in our lives as real and present with us. This may seem very personal and open to criticism. However, it is the experience of Jesus being truly alive and with us spiritually that is the most wonderful thing about being a Christian. My experience of him at my own conversion was as real as the chair I am sitting on.

Actually, at first, I had my doubts of whether this knowledge of his presence would last. It has done—and I was once one of the world's greatest sceptics.

Such a personal experience, repeated in so many people, is real and unique.

---

[114] John7:5

Summing up the evidence

Anyone with an open mind who really engages with this evidence must come to the conclusion that Jesus did indeed rise physically from the dead.

Sir Norman Anderson, a Professor of Law, looked at all the evidence and wrote showing that Jesus must have risen from the grave[115]. In his book, he writes:

"Either the resurrection is infinitely more than a beautiful story, or it is infinitely less. If it is true, then it is the supreme fact of history; and to fail to adjust one's life to its implications means irreparable loss."

---

[115] Anderson J.N.D. (1950). The evidence of the Resurrection. IVP

APPENDIX

The age of the earth

One of the issues that divides some Christians is the age of the earth. There are those who feel that the straightforward reading of Genesis requires us to believe that the earth is only a few thousand years old. Others feel that Genesis does not require this, and that science has shown us that the earth and the universe are billions of years old.

There is the history of a similar controversy in the 17th century which dramatically divided Christians. Galileo had discovered that the earth goes around the sun. Psalm 104:5 says: *He set the earth on its foundations; it can never be moved.* And so, Galileo was forced to recant for heresy and put under house arrest. We now know that we do not need to believe in a fixed unmoving earth to believe in the Bible's authority. This verse is not about the earth's movement in space but about its stability—something quite different.

No one nowadays believes the sun goes around the earth. But what of the age of the earth? There is a lot of pain and dispute over this. Why is this unnecessary? While I am giving a considered opinion here, I respect those fellow Christians who cannot accept a very ancient Earth and do so out of reverence for the Bible.

Biblical interpretation

There is misunderstanding about the beginning of the six days of creation. Each day begins with *"And God said…"* But the first day begins in verse 3. The first two verses, which involve the creation of the *'heavens and the earth'* if we read it literally, are about the time *before* the first day. Moreover, the tense used in the first two verses is a past tense, different from that used in the rest of the days of creation. Therefore, there is no actual time period given for when the *'heavens and the earth'* were created. It is indefinite. It could have been thousands or billions of years. The Bible therefore says nothing about the age of the earth and universe.

It is also very hard to reconcile the order of the creation of the sun and moon with 24-hour day in a time sequence. It is only on the 4th day (verses 14-19) that the sun and moon are created in this narrative. The 24-hour day depends on the sun. Yet, there have already been 3 'days' and, in verses 3 to 5, the separation of light and darkness into day and night. It is a very strained interpretation therefore that takes the days as being one after the other in sequence.

One valid way of seeing the days (and there are other ways) is not so much in order of an actual time sequence but in what can be called a 'framework' view.[116] The first three days sum up the universality of creation, including light and darkness, water and air, land and vegetation. The last three sum up the particulars—sun, moon, fish and birds, animals and humanity.

What Genesis *does* say beautifully is that the universe and the earth were created by God who is exalted and supreme. And, as has been shown in this book, it was all created from nothing.

And so, a thorough reverence for the authority of scripture is possible without insisting on a particular age of the universe or the earth.

The science

Much of this book has discussed the science which now overwhelmingly indicates a great age of the universe and the earth. We can now measure the distance to galaxies far away and we know that the light from them has taken billions of years to reach us. We also know a great deal about dating the earth—particularly from the study of radioactive isotopes which decay at a very steady and known rate.

It seems to me that we should look to good science to get our ideas of how God formed this wonderful universe.

We could do here with a lesson from Augustine, over 1500 years ago, who was very clear in stating that

---

[116] This is the view of John Lennox. See Lennox, John. (2011). Seven Days that Divide the World. Zondervan

165

Christians need to be careful not to give biblical interpretations of science which those outside the church know to be wrong. For Augustine, this was dangerous to our mission in winning people to the truth. He wrote:

The shame is not so much that an ignorant individual is derided, but that people outside the household of faith think our sacred writers held such opinions, and, to the great loss of those for whose salvation we toil, the writers of our Scripture are criticized and rejected as unlearned men.[117]

---

[117] Augustine: The Literal Meaning of Genesis. Book 1, Chapter 19, Paragraph 39.